# BATTLEFIELD
# WALKS
## NORTH

# BATTLEFIELD
# WALKS
## NORTH

*David Clark*

Grange
BOOKS

A Sutton Publishing Book

This edition published in 1997 by Grange Books
An imprint of Grange Books plc
The Grange
Grange Yard
London SE1 3AG

ISBN 1-84013-008-3

This book was designed and produced by
Alan Sutton Publishing Limited, an imprint of Sutton Publishing Limited,
Phoenix Mill, Thrupp, Stroud, Gloucestershire, GL5 2BU

Typeset in 11/12 Plantin Light.
Typesetting and origination by
Sutton Publishing Limited.
Printed in Great Britain by
WBC Limited, Bridgend.

# CONTENTS

List of Illustrations     vii

List of Maps     ix

General Map showing location of the walks     x

Introduction     xi

1  The Battle of Stamford Bridge (1066)     1

2  The Battle of the Standard (1138)     13

3  The Battle of Boroughbridge (1322)     25

4  The Battle of Neville's Cross (1346)     37

5  The Battle of Otterburn (1388)     50

6  The Battle of Towton (1461)     62

7  The Battle of Hexham (1464)     76

8  The Battle of Flodden (1513)     89

9  The Battle of Newburn (1640)     101

10  The Siege of York (1644)     112

11  The Battle of Marston Moor (1644)     125

12  RAF Marston Moor (1941–5)     138

Further Reading     151

Index of Places     155

Index of Persons     159

# LIST OF ILLUSTRATIONS

| | | |
|---|---|---|
| 1. | Halley's Comet | 3 |
| 2. | The Shallows, Stamford Bridge | 5 |
| 3. | David I of Scotland | 15 |
| 4. | Scotpit Lane | 17 |
| 5. | The Battlefield Monument, Northallerton | 22 |
| 6. | Boroughbridge | 29 |
| 7. | The Battle Cross, Aldborough | 34 |
| 8. | The capture of David II | 39 |
| 9. | Durham Cathedral | 42 |
| 10. | Neville's Cross | 47 |
| 11. | Greenchesters | 53 |
| 12. | The Douglas Pennon | 54 |
| 13. | Percy's Cross | 55 |
| 14. | Site map of the Battle of Otterburn | 59 |
| 15. | Edward IV | 65 |
| 16. | Lord Dacre's Tomb | 67 |
| 17. | Lord Dacre's Cross | 72 |
| 18. | The Marriage of Henry VI and Margaret of Anjou | 78 |
| 19. | Hexham Abbey Church and Market Place | 82 |
| 20. | Flodden Field | 93 |
| 21. | The Standard of the Earl Marischal of Scotland | 94 |
| 22. | The Battlefield Monument, Branxton | 98 |
| 23. | General Alexander Leslie | 103 |
| 24. | Newburn Bridge | 105 |
| 25. | Clifford's Tower | 113 |
| 26. | Seventeenth-century York | 122 |
| 27. | Cromwell's Plump | 128 |
| 28. | White Syke Close | 135 |
| 29. | WAAF Officers' Mess, RAF Marston Moor | 140 |
| 30. | A Handley Page Halifax II (W7676 TL–P) | 142 |
| 31. | Aircraft sheds, RAF Marston Moor | 147 |

# LIST OF MAPS

| | | |
|---|---|---|
| 1. | Battlefield sites in the North | xiii |
| 2. | Stamford Bridge | 8 |
| 3. | Northallerton | 20 |
| 4. | Boroughbridge | 32 |
| 5. | Neville's Cross | 46 |
| 6. | Otterburn | 58 |
| 7. | Towton | 70 |
| 8. | Hexham | 85 |
| 9. | Flodden | 96 |
| 10. | Newburn | 108 |
| 11. | York | 120 |
| 12. | Marston Moor | 132 |
| 13. | RAF Marston Moor | 146 |

**Battlefield Walks
North**

# INTRODUCTION

The North of England has much to offer the battlefield historian, with the sites of over a dozen fierce encounters spread unevenly over the land between the Humber and the Tyne. A few of the names – Stamford Bridge (1066), Flodden (1513) and Marston Moor (1644) – are well known, while others such as Hexham (1464) and Newburn (1640), having failed to capture the popular imagination, have faded into relative obscurity. In fact, a book built upon a discussion of selected battles is always liable to attract criticism regarding the reasons for certain omissions and, likewise, the justification for particular inclusions.

For instance, although the present volume opens on the eve of the Norman Conquest, with the Battle of Stamford Bridge, it ignores many significant battles which had been fought in the North of England during the previous millennium. So, there is no mention of the fighting which occurred during the Roman occupation, nor of the battles in the centuries of civil war which followed the Roman withdrawal, or of the years of Viking raids which preceded the Norman invasion.

The problem with the entire period is the paucity of information available to anyone who is so rash as to attempt a detailed analysis. Even the sites of the battles remain frustratingly elusive. So, for example, the Battle of Chester can be described only as occurring around the year 615, while the Battle of Degsastan (603) may or may not have taken place in Liddesdale – and so on.

A further difficulty which besets anyone attempting to design an informative and attractive walk based upon a battlefield is the issue of accessibility. Exploration of the sites of such well-known battles as the Wars of the Roses clash at Wakefield (1460) and the English Civil War battle at Preston (1648) is not feasible because of the transformation of what were once rural landscapes into urban sprawls.

In addition, although some battlefields have been lucky enough to escape development, there may yet be restraints on access, in terms of a lack of public footpath facilities. Although the Landranger and Pathfinder series of Ordnance Survey maps constitute an invaluable aid in this respect, they identify many footpaths which no longer exist – an observation which is intended to be a criticism of those local authorities whose responsibility it is to maintain the paths in question, as opposed to casting aspersions upon the accuracy of Ordnance Survey reporting. Unfortunately, several illustrations of this growing problem are to be found throughout this volume.

Some good news for the reflective rambler is that the major battlefields of the North of England are to be found grouped together. This is in contradistinction to battlefields of the South of England, the Midlands and Scotland, which are more widely dispersed. Thus, for example, it is possible, within the context of an entertaining – and rewarding – short holiday in the vicinity of York, to explore Stamford Bridge, Marston Moor and the Civil War defences of the city itself.

The key to understanding the outcome of many battles, including most of those described in the present volume, lies in an appreciation of the local landscape. When forced on to the defensive, an army with its back to a river could meet a watery end. On the other hand, the advantage conferred by the occupation of high ground might prove decisive. But, whatever the nature of the topographical considerations, the point to note is that a visit to the site in question is invaluable for helping one to arrive at a considered judgement of the reasons why a battle was won or lost. Therefore, the sketch maps included in each section are unencumbered with contour lines or hachures – a discussion of the role of topographical features in each battle being limited to the section describing the suggested walk.

Although the Ordnance Survey Pathfinder maps clearly identify the public footpaths and bridle-ways crossing farmland which are used in the walks, it is often advisable as a matter of courtesy – particularly, for example, when the route crosses a farmyard – to have a preliminary word with the farmer.

No attempt has been made to estimate the time needed for the completion of the walks because so much depends upon the topography, the pace of the individual rambler, and the extent to which one is agreeably side-tracked by complementary distractions. In a world dominated by the necessity of stringent timekeeping, it is a luxury to allow oneself to lose all sense of time in stepping out into an exploration of 600 years of colourful and exciting history.

# 1
# THE BATTLE OF STAMFORD BRIDGE
## 25 September 1066

## *Introduction*

King Edward I of England, popularly known as 'the Confessor' and usually described as a pious half-wit, reigned over England from 1042 to 1066. He owed his position to the powerful Godwin family, which imported him from Normandy where he had been living in exile for thirty years. Edward's major – and only – qualification for the job lay in his descent from Alfred the Great. The shrewd Godwins foresaw that the combination of Edward's impeccable pedigree and patent unworldliness would both unite the country and enable them to get on with the serious business of running it.

From the beginning, the arrangement proved a success, Edward busying himself with self-purification, while the House of Godwin concerned itself with affairs of state. There was only one problem which tended to put a strain on the agreement: Edward's Norman connections. As the reign progressed, a 'fifth column' of Norman clerics, administrators and landowners became absorbed into the infrastructure of Anglo-Saxon society – thus paving the way for a smooth transition to power, whenever the opportunity for military conquest should arise.

At one point, Earl Godwin, the family patriarch, was driven into exile through devious Norman machinations. During his enforced absence, Edward may well have promised the English crown to William, Duke of Normandy. Shortly after his successful return, Earl Godwin died. The power vacuum was filled by his eldest son, Harold, who quarrelled with his pro-Norman brother, Tostig.

Preservation of the unity of the realm became – and remained – Harold's top priority. In fact, he had dedicated himself to a lost cause, for Saxon England was a society in irreversible decline. It was a process hastened by the

Godwins themselves. In parcelling-out great tracts of land to their favourites, they had fostered the creation of a country of largely independent earldoms, with little allegiance to central authority. Indeed, chieftains of these minor principalities were soon presiding over their own courts, thus diverting income from fines away from the royal exchequer and into their own pockets.

In the traditional Saxon strongholds of the south and west, a servile peasantry – one of the distinguishing features of the feudal system – was becoming established. On the other hand, in East Anglia and the north-west, both areas of heavy Scandinavian settlement, feudalism evolved rather more slowly, which all added to the general picture of fragmentation and disunity.

In continental Europe, expansionist warlords cast covetous glances across the Channel upon this decaying Saxon kingdom which would shortly be ripe for conquest. The time for action arrived on 5 January 1066, when Edward died peacefully in his own Westminster Abbey. It is said that his final act was to nominate Harold as his successor. Certainly, Harold lost no time in regularizing the situation for, on the day of Edward's funeral – 6 January – he was crowned King of England.

If it were still possible to patch up the decaying fabric of Saxon England, then Harold, the antithesis of his predecessor, was the man to do it – by force, if necessary. His skills as a military commander were beyond doubt and he was at liberty to call on the services of a small standing army known as the 'house-carls'. Formed in the reign of Canute, the house-carls were a body of highly trained, paid soldiers. Well equipped with axe, javelin and sword, this élite corps of professionals prided itself on its mobility and versatility – attributes which were to be tested to the full during the dark days of Harold's short and violent reign.

Upon his deathbed, Edward had prophesied that evil would soon fall upon the land. In an ultra-superstitious age, such words did not fall on deaf ears, and men eagerly scanned the heavens, looking for a sign which might be interpreted as God's seal of approval on the choice of Harold as sovereign. The sign came immediately after Easter, with the appearance, in clear skies, of Halley's Comet. A fiery sword, blazing defiantly in the firmament, its appearance was widely interpreted as signifying not God's pleasure, but His anger at Harold's usurpation of the crown. It was a bad omen.

# The Road to Stamford Bridge

The sightings of Halley's Comet in 1066 extended far beyond the British Isles, and the significance of its timely appearance, as interpreted by soothsayers throughout Western Europe, was not lost on the vultures waiting

Halley's Comet. The arrival of Halley's Comet, as depicted here in the Bayeux Tapestry, so soon after Harold's coronation was considered by many to be a bad omen. It seems to have been generally accepted that Harold had sworn fealty to William of Normandy and that the appearance of this blazing sword in the sky was a sign of God's displeasure at what was seen as a betrayal of trust. The event was exploited by the lunatic fringe and prophecies of impending doom and disaster were spread far and wide. (Mansell Collection)

patiently in the wings for an opportunity to tear asunder the rotting carcase of Saxon sovereignty.

Foremost among these voracious predators were William, Duke of Normandy, and Harold Hardrada, King of Norway. Both were courted by the new English monarch's brother, Tostig. For some months, Tostig had been living in exile. Having been deprived of the Earldom of Northumbria, following accusations of misrule, he had broken with his elder brother and decamped to Flanders, where he devoted himself to plotting Harold's downfall.

After being rebuffed by the King of Denmark, who appeared uninterested in any scheme for invasion, Tostig turned his attention to William, only to find that he had plans of his own. So, it was left to the disgruntled exile to mount an expedition of his own, a paltry affair which degenerated into a series of raids along the Kent coastline. He did succeed in capturing Sandwich, then an important naval base – an action which forced Harold's hand. By the time he reached Sandwich, however, Tostig had moved on to pastures new, mounting assaults on the east coast from Norfolk to Yorkshire. Unfortunately, the further north he sailed, the more redoubtable became the resistance of the local militia. At length, most of his men, satiated with plunder, drew off, leaving him to run for cover to Scotland, where King Malcolm gave him shelter. It was during his sojourn in Scotland that Tostig acquired the support of Hardrada of Norway.

Harold guessed that large-scale invasion schemes were afoot. He anticipated attacks from both Norway and Normandy, but he had no way of knowing which would happen first. It all depended upon the prevailing winds. Throughout the early summer of 1066, those winds swept down from the north, favouring Tostig and his Norwegian allies. And yet, having calculated that the Northumbrians were well able to defend themselves, Harold travelled south, amassing his army on the Isle of Wight where he remained until September, waiting in vain for the wind to change.

Taking advantage of the circumstances which kept William tied up in port, Hardrada crossed to the Orkneys (at that time dependencies of Norway) at the beginning of August. By the end of the month, reinforced by Tostig and Scottish mercenaries, the invasion force may have numbered as many as 9,000 men. Setting sail, this formidable array proceeded to wreak havoc along the north-east coastline before turning in to the River Humber. Pressing on into the Ouse – and, doubtless, striking terror into the hearts of all who witnessed its passage – the fleet finally came to rest to the south of York, at Riccall.

In the second week of September with the north winds continuing unabated, Harold had been compelled to disband his army. Returning to the mainland, he marched with his regulars to London, where he learned of the Norwegian landings. With the benefit of hindsight, he would have been well advised to remain in the north, where the threat posed by Hardrada was proving to be more serious than he had anticipated. On 20 September, therefore, he set out on the 200 mile trek to York where Morcar, Tostig's replacement as Earl of Northumberland, had cobbled together an army to repel the invaders.

Unwisely, Morcar met the Norwegians head-on 2 miles to the south of York, at Fulford. In a brief but fierce encounter, in which there were heavy casualties on both sides, the English force was soundly beaten, and Hardrada was able to dictate his own terms. These were surprisingly generous. In exchange for hostages and supplies, York – then the third most important city in the country – would not be sacked. The citizens agreed to meet the invaders at Stamford Bridge, 8 miles to the east, on 25 September, when both hostages and provisions would be handed over.

What the Norwegians could not know was that on 24 September, after one of the most famous forced marches of all time, Harold arrived at

Tadcaster, having covered almost 200 miles in just five days. In the early hours of the following day, he entered York, where he was appraised of the situation. Almost immediately, at the head of 4,000 men, he struck out for Stamford Bridge where Hardrada, with up to two-thirds of his army – in excess of 5,000 men – was waiting patiently for his tribute.

# The Battle of Stamford Bridge

In 1066 Stamford Bridge consisted of nothing more than a bridge, a wooden structure which was so narrow that it could be used by only one or two men at a time. Several roads converge to effect a crossing of the River Derwent at this point, and it was for this reason that the Norwegians selected it as an outpost. Perhaps they did not anticipate Harold's approach from the west. It may be that they did not expect him at all, but the rapid approach of the English on the morning of 25 September caught them at a disadvantage on the west bank.

The Shallows, Stamford Bridge. This is one possible location of the wooden bridge which crossed the River Derwent in 1066. Another is a little upstream, about 50 yards beyond the present-day weir.

The land on each side of the river rises to a ridge. Hardrada and Tostig withdrew the greater portion of their force to the east ridge, a smaller body being drawn up on the west bank to cover the retreat and to defend the bridge.

The English, showing no signs of fatigue following their forced march, bore down upon the invaders who, despite selling their lives dearly, were eventually swamped by sheer weight of numbers. At length, there remained only one Norwegian on the bridge. A gigantic fellow armed with a double-headed axe, he held his position – according to some accounts – for several hours, repelling all efforts to dislodge him. In the end, he was defeated only by subterfuge. Apparently, an English soldier managed to acquire a swill-tub (a trough for feeding hogs), using it to float under the bridge and despatch the worthy Horatius with an upward spear-thrust.

Instead of remaining close to the bridge, the numerically superior Norwegian contingent on the east bank fell back to higher ground, specifically to the area now known as Battle Flats, where the main conflict took place. Thus, the English were permitted to complete their crossing of the river and to launch an attack on what had been developed into a strong defensive position.

The Norwegians were drawn up in a horseshoe-shaped formation, Tostig and Hardrada, each with his personal retinue, occupying the centre. It is doubtful whether cavalry played a prominent role in the fighting. Against a seemingly impregnable wall of tightly packed Norwegian shields, a mounted assault would have been of limited value. In such situations, mounted men were used to probe for weaknesses in the shield-wall in an effort to create an opening for their infantry.

At some indeterminate stage – possibly now – Harold offered generous peace terms to Tostig. When these were rejected, the English launched their attack. According to some sources – largely discredited – the Norwegians mounted a counter-offensive of their own. In reality, however, it was all they could do to hold their ground before the determined English advance as, inch by inch, the house-carls, with Harold at their head, pressed forward. Gradually, an increasing number of gaps appeared in the Norwegian defences, with the concentrated fighting breaking up into a series of small-group and individual combats.

With an occasional lull, this bruising contest went on for the better part of the day, and men on both sides must have been dropping from exhaustion. An input of fresh troops would have proved decisive. Harold had no hope of reinforcements, but the Norwegians knew that help would be on the way from their base-camp at Riccall. Unfortunately, the Norwegian reserves were so exhausted when they arrived that they proved unequal to the task. It is said that they were so fatigued by their march that they threw off their chain-mail, so falling easy prey to sword and axe. Although the tide of battle did turn briefly in favour of the invaders, the English held on.

Eventually, Hardrada was felled by one of the comparatively few English archers on the field, while a house-carl's axe split Tostig's skull down to the jaw-bone. With the death of their leaders, Norwegian resistance collapsed and, despite their own weariness, the victors began a long and bloody pursuit of the enemy, now fleeing in panic to the temporary safety of their fleet.

# The Aftermath

For Harold and the English, it was a stunning victory. Taking into account Fulford, Stamford Bridge and the slaughter which followed, it is fairly certain that upwards of 5,000 Norwegians perished on English soil. Whereas the invasion force had required 300 troop-ships, only twenty-four were needed to ferry home the survivors, the remainder of the once-proud Armada being put to the torch. The lives of Prince Olaf and the Earl of Orkney were spared so that each could recount the sorry tale to his fellow-countrymen. On behalf of their respective nations, both pledged never again to bear arms against England – a promise that the Norwegians, at least, have honoured to this day.

Of the enemy dead, those of high rank received decent burials. The bodies of the common soldiers were left to rot where they lay as Harold made arrangements for a triumphal entry to York where, laden with hostages and booty, he planned to consolidate his position. In this connection, there was much to do. After any great battle, the victor proves his true worth by the skill with which he manages the peace process. As is customary, quarrels were breaking out among the victors about the division of the spoils in terms of land, titles and treasure – much of the latter commodity belonging, by rights, to the civilians from whom it had been stolen.

And then there was the tradition of the post-battle celebrations to uphold – feasting at long tables in the great Saxon halls, lit by flaming torches from which wreaths of smoke curled upwards to the wooden rafters of the high, vaulted ceilings – raucous functions of several days' duration at which the fighting men would eat and drink themselves into insensibility.

At this point, the story should end. In fact, it was just beginning for, on 28 September 1066, just three days after Stamford Bridge, William, Duke of Normandy, landed at Pevensey. The story is often told of how the victory banquet was interrupted by the arrival of a messenger with the news. In fact, Harold had been conscious throughout of the imminent peril on the south coast, and he may well have been en route to London when the intelligence reached him.

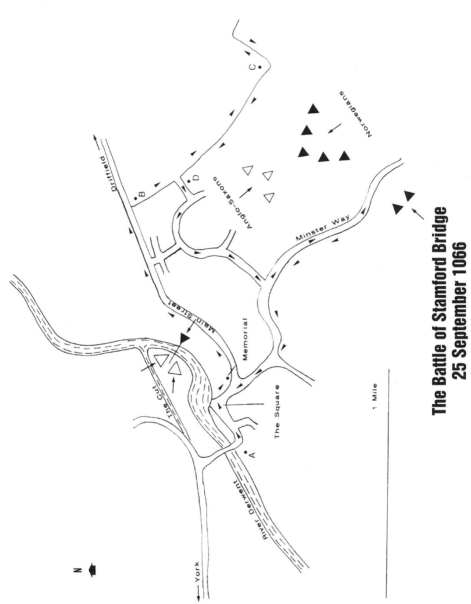

The Battle of Stamford Bridge
25 September 1066

It was at the subsequent Battle of Hastings that the long-term results of Stamford Bridge were felt. The English losses at both Stamford Bridge and Fulford left the ranks of seasoned campaigners sadly depleted. In addition, the surviving veterans, many with wounds, were in the process of chalking up what would amount to a total of nearly 500 miles in forced marches. Any attempt to handle two invasions, at opposite ends of the country, within so short a space of time, was bound to end in defeat. Indeed, with some justification, it may be argued that Harold's brilliant victory at Stamford Bridge facilitated the Norman Conquest of England.

# The Walk

**Distance:** 4¾ miles (7.64 km)

Begin at the picnic site on the south side of the present-day bridge (point A; Pathfinder 665 712555). Cross over The Square to the village green to view a display board containing a descriptive battle plan. Adjacent to the green is The Shallows section of the Derwent. The Stamford Bridge of the battle may have stood a little further upstream above the weir. In all probability, the river was fordable over The Shallows, and the wooden bridge – if one existed – would have been adjacent to it.

Of course, if there was no bridge, then the tale concerning the fate of the Norwegian who held it is relegated to the realms of fantasy. However, the story survived in a celebration, called the 'Spear Pie Feast', which lasted well into the last quarter of the nineteenth century. As part of the celebrations, which took place each September, boat-shaped pies bearing the impression of a spear would be baked.

Return to the road and walk up Main Street. On a mound opposite the Bay Horse inn is a stone memorial with an inscription to the effect that the battle was 'fought in this neighbourhood'. Continue walking along Main Street, out of the village and on to the A166 road to Driffield.

The walk out of the village is longer than it used to be owing to the addition of a modern housing estate on the right-hand side of the road. Built squarely across the Norwegian line of retreat to Battle Flats, the development has not added to the ambience of this important historical site.

Continue along the A166 until attaining the public footpath at the end of the estate (point B; Pathfinder 665 718559). Adjacent uncultivated land would suggest that the building programme is to be extended. Follow this path which develops into a farm track, leading into what was probably an area of heavy fighting. Where the track veers to the left (point C; Pathfinder 665 724555) pause, look around and try to envisage the battlefield as it would have appeared to the combatants.

Ahead, the land rises towards the Yorkshire Wolds. The Norwegians may have felt that the gentle gradient would have given them an edge against Harold's men marching up from the river. To the right is the undulating country across which the weary Norwegian relief column would have had to struggle in their dash from Riccall. Down through the centuries, swords, spears and horseshoes have been unearthed on this land, just as fragments of weaponry have been recovered from the Derwent.

In 1958, on the occasion of the author's first visit to Stamford Bridge, it was possible to walk across the battlefield by means of a public footpath which has long since disappeared. An alternative route, which was intended to replace the original, has fallen into disuse, and it is necessary, therefore, to retrace one's steps to the housing estate.

Instead of returning to the road, take a left turn into the estate at Garrowby View (point D). Turn right into Burton Fields Road and then bear left into Battleflats Way. This road eventually links up with the Wilberfoss road, which is now part of a medium-distance footpath called the Minster Way, running between Beverley and York. Turn left into the Minster Way in order to obtain a view of the Battle Flats area – as marked on the Pathfinder 510 – which, again, would have been the scene of fierce fighting, particularly after the arrival of the Norwegian reserves.

Turn back and follow the road back into Stamford Bridge and the picnic area starting-point on the left.

# Further Explorations

A little over 7 miles to the north-west of Stamford Bridge is the village of Sheriff Hutton (Landranger 100 6566), site of a ruined castle which once stood at the heart of the nation's affairs. Built by Bertram de Bulmer in the reign of King Stephen, its name denotes the appointment of de Bulmer as Sheriff of Yorkshire. During the years of conflict between Stephen and Matilda, it remained one of Stephen's strongholds. Later, it passed, through marriage, to the Neville family. Ralph Neville, who was to transfer his allegiance from Richard II to Henry of Bolingbroke, embarked on a rebuilding programme which saw the castle both extended and fortified.

The Nevilles kept the castle for 300 years, until the death of the Earl of Warwick, 'The Kingmaker' at the Battle of Barnet in 1471, when the estate was given by Edward IV to Richard, Duke of Gloucester, the future Richard III, for whom Sheriff Hutton Castle always held a special appeal. Richard used the castle as a prison for Anthony Woodville and Elizabeth of York. Woodville (Earl Rivers) ultimately lost his head at Pontefract Castle, while Elizabeth became Henry VII's queen, the union uniting the Houses of York and Lancaster.

Henry VII, retaining the castle as crown property, then gave it to Thomas Howard, Duke of Norfolk as a residence for the duration of his lifetime. When Norfolk died, it was used by Henry Fitzroy, Duke of Richmond, who held the office of Lieutenant General of the North. This period proved to be the castle's swan-song for, soon afterwards, it fell into a state of disrepair and neglect. Gradually, it was dismantled by local people, its stone utilized in the construction of rather more modest local dwellings – some of which can still be seen in the village today.

The remains of Sheriff Hutton's Church of St Helen are largely fourteenth century. It is said that Edward, the only son of Richard III and his queen, Anne, who died at Middleham Castle in 1484, was buried here. On what is allegedly his tomb within the church stands an alabaster representation of the young prince in an attitude of prayer.

The village of Full Sutton lies 2 miles to the east of Stamford Bridge. Attached to it was one of the last Second World War airfields to be opened in Yorkshire (Landranger 105 7454). A heavy bomber station, it came into operation in May 1944 and the Halifax bombers flew many missions over the course of the ensuing twelve months. In 1947 it closed – only to reopen in 1951 in response to the conflict in Korea. In the late 1950s, following a period as a USAAF reserve site, the RAF again took it over for use as a base for Thor missiles. As with many Second World War airfields, Full Sutton looked set to end its days as a make-shift industrial estate. In the early 1980s, however, it was confirmed that plans were afoot to build what is now Full Sutton prison on the site.

An effort should be made to visit Riccall (Landranger 105 6237), Hardrada's main campsite in the run-up to the Battle of Stamford Bridge. By covering the distance between the two sites, one can appreciate the reason for the weariness of the Norwegian reserves upon their arrival at Battle Flats. The Ouse twists and turns rather more than it did in Hardrada's time, but Riccall Landing (Pathfinder 685 608374) has undergone little change since the days when the Norwegian fleet was moored here.

Fulford (Landranger 105 6149), where Hardrada overcame the first English army sent against him, is now a suburb of York. Gritty English resistance was overcome by a well timed and ferocious Norwegian assault, many of the retreating English being cut down in the marshes bordering the river (Pathfinder 674 607493).

# Further Information

The Battle of Stamford Bridge has always tended to be overshadowed by the Battle of Hastings. An account of the battle and of events leading up to it may be found in Volume I of William Seymour's *Battles in Britain*, with other readable accounts in Barrett's *Battles and Battlefields in England* and Leadman's *Battles Fought in Yorkshire*. As is often the case, locally obtainable publications fill the gap – notably Roger Wordsworth's *The Battle of Stamford Bridge and the Northern Campaign of 1066* and Jessie K. Payne's *Stamford Bridge: The Story of the Battle and Historical Notes on the Village*.

Landranger 105 and Pathfinder 665 are the relevant Ordnance Survey maps, although both are currently (1994) a little out of date.

Stamford Bridge lies 7 miles to the east of York, on the A166 and, with York encircled by a ring road, is easily accessible from all directions. During the summer months, delays can occur at the bridge, which is restricted to one-way traffic, controlled by traffic-lights.

Travellers by rail should head for York (tel: 01904 642155) and complete their journey by bus (tel. 01904 624161). Stamford Bridge is also well served via the National Express coach network on the London–Whitby route (tel: 0171 730 0202) and the Swansea–Scarborough route (tel: 01792 470820).

For refreshments, try The Swordsman – its sign depicting the untimely end of the heroic Norwegian who held the bridge – or, in the summer, the gardens of The Corn Mill, by the weir.

# 2
# THE BATTLE OF THE STANDARD
## 22 August 1138

## *Introduction*

Of the Battle of the Standard, the eminent military historian A.H. Burne states that 'its interest is so predominantly ecclesiastical rather than military that it is worth no more than a brief and cursory description'. Alternatively, Philip Warner, in his British Battlefields series, argues that it was 'one of the most extraordinary battles in English history'. William Seymour's classic *Battles in Britain* ignores it altogether, whereas Peter Young and John Adair's *From Hastings to Culloden*, although declining to recognize it as a major battle, allows that it 'certainly merits our attention'.

The major protagonists involved in the Battle of the Standard (or 'Northallerton' as it is sometimes called) are not 'popular' historical figures. For example, of all English monarchs, King Stephen must be one of the least well known, although he reigned for twenty turbulent years. William the Conqueror had three legitimate sons and one daughter. The eldest son, Robert, spent his days fomenting trouble in Normandy and so, when the conqueror died, the second eldest son, William II ('William Rufus') succeeded. He was followed by the third son, who became Henry I. The daughter, Adela, married Stephen, Count of Blois, and it was her son, also named Stephen, who usurped the throne on Henry's death.

By virtue of his direct descent from the Conqueror, Stephen did have a claim to the crown. Henry's only son, Robert, had drowned at sea when the royal yacht struck a rock off the coast of Normandy. However, there was a daughter, Matilda, and Henry set his heart on her ruling as queen after his death. While some barons were prepared to accept her, many others looked askance at the prospect of giving allegiance to a woman – capable though she might be. In this division of opinion lay the seeds of a bloody civil war.

When Henry died, both Stephen and Matilda were in Normandy, Stephen in Brittany and Matilda further inland, in Anjou. Thus, Stephen was able to cross the Channel and, with the help of his brother, Henry of

Blois, seize the treasury and persuade the Archbishop of Canterbury to anoint him. In order to secure the support he needed, Stephen had to promise to make concessions to the church and the baronage, for his father had developed a strong, central administration at the expense of both. In the spring of 1836, therefore, Stephen issued a 'charter of liberties' in which he confirmed all the ancient customs and privileges enjoyed by the Church at the time of William the Conqueror's death. He also guaranteed to restore to the Church all its lands sequestered by Henry. The bishops, for their part, swore fealty to him for so long as he adhered to his promises.

Under Henry, the barons had been kept firmly in check. The creation of an Exchequer and the central appointment and management of sheriffs, responsible for the collection of monies accruing to the Crown, diminished baronial independence and freedom of action. The final years of Henry's reign had witnessed growing tension between Crown and baronage, the king being recognized as a champion of the peasantry, shielding it from the worst excesses of feudalism. To some extent, Stephen had been carried to power on a tidal wave of baronial reaction against Henry's autocratic tendencies, and he was expected to repay this support with the imposition of a milder form of government.

In short, in order to acquire the Crown, Stephen had to sacrifice the very principles of government which made for a strong monarchy. By devolving power upon his supporters, he was storing up for himself future trouble, for his friends recognized in him a certain weakness of character which they planned, in the course of time, to turn to their own advantage.

# The Road to Northallerton

A united Anglo-Norman kingdom often led to difficulties in Normandy overshadowing problems nearer 'home'. Having been beaten to the finishing post in the race for the Crown, Matilda soon turned her attention to consolidating her own position in Normandy. Upon Henry's death, some strongholds on the southern border had been handed over to her, and she now hoped to use them as a basis for extending her influence. Unfortunately, her husband, Geoffrey of Anjou, hated the Normans to such an extent that Matilda was deprived of much potential support, so when Stephen crossed the Channel in March 1137, the question of Norman allegiance still hung in the balance.

Such advantages as Stephen possessed were rapidly thrown away when, in planning a punitive expedition against Geoffrey and Matilda, he alienated the Normans by his insistence on using Flemish mercenaries. For this reason, the offensive never took place and, having forfeited Norman trust, Stephen was compelled to make a truce with his rivals.

In England, Stephen's behaviour also did little to inspire confidence. Always seemingly on the defensive, his lack of foresight and determination leaves one wondering how he had managed to act so decisively in taking the Crown. Rebellions broke out simultaneously in several parts of the country. In particular, Baldwin de Redvers, the only leading baron who had refused to give fealty to Stephen, took Exeter Castle which managed to withstand a three months' siege. When the garrison did surrender, de Redvers' fellow barons insisted that the rebels should go free. De Redvers himself then proceeded to raise a pirate fleet which, from a base on the Isle of Wight, preyed on the commerce of Portsmouth and Southampton. When, eventually, de Redvers fled to Anjou, it became plain for all to see that Geoffrey and Matilda had backed his insurrection from the outset.

A leading light of the Angevin conspiracy was Robert of Gloucester. A bastard son of Henry I, he remained fiercely loyal to Matilda, and to the furtherance of her cause he devoted all his wealth and influence. As a result of Stephen's incompetent handling of the Normandy situation, Robert was able to use the province as a base for plotting and scheming. His supporters in England, meanwhile, contented themselves with extending the defences of their castles – for this was the great age of fortification when sieges began to play as important a role in warfare as pitched battles.

Another problem for Stephen was that of the ever-present danger of invasions from both Wales and Scotland. The Scottish king, David I, had

David I of Scotland. The Scottish king was soundly beaten at the Battle of the Standard, but still managed to secure a handsome settlement with the acquisition for his son, Prince Henry, of the Earldom of Northumbria. (National Galleries Scotland)

long been a supporter of Matilda, if only because it provided him with an excuse for mounting border raids. In 1136, in an unwise attempt at appeasement, Stephen had ceded Cumbria to Scotland – which encouraged David to seek further concessions by making more forays across the border. Even at the time – in an age of hardship – these raids were noted for their excessive brutality and savagery. Under the smoke-screen they created, revolt broke out in the south of England, with Robert of Gloucester's rebel barons – holding many of the strongest castles in the country – throwing down the gauntlet.

Stephen was reduced to attacking each stronghold in turn. Somehow he contrived to ignore Bristol Castle, the key to the Earldom of Gloucester – and the greater part of Robert's resources. And yet, in the scattered nature of the revolt lay its weakness as well as its strength, for the rebel barons were unable to join forces to meet Stephen in the field. This honour went to King David who, in the summer of 1138, crossed the frontier at Carlisle, at the head of an army of 12,000 men – a mongrel host comprising Scots, disaffected English, Norwegians, Normans, Germans and Danes. Clearly, this was no ordinary raiding party.

# The Battle of the Standard

Stephen, attending to the rebellion in the south, was in no position to address the problems in the north. Unmolested, David was able to ravage Northumberland before pressing on into North Yorkshire. At length, the northern barons, prepared to sink their differences in order to meet the threat posed by a common enemy, organized some resistance. The effort was coordinated by Archbishop Thurstan of York, who also held the office of Lieutenant of the North. Bearer of the King's Commission, which gave the seal of approval to the cause, was Bernard de Balliol, additional prominent support being lent by Walter L'Espec, the Sheriff of Yorkshire and William le Gros, Earl of Albermarle – the builder of the impregnable Scarborough Castle.

The scratch English force marched from York to Thirsk, where it halted while Balliol parleyed with the invaders. David's justification for the invasion revolved around Scottish claims upon the old Earldom of Northumbria. It is said that Balliol, presumably working to Stephen's instructions, offered the earldom to David's son, Prince Henry, but that the Scottish king, interpreting these efforts at conciliation as a demonstration of weakness, laughed in his face. So, Balliol withdrew and the English, perhaps 10,000 men in all, marched on to Northallerton and beyond – to an area of gently rising ground 3 miles out of the town, on the Darlington road.

Here, at dawn on 22 August, was raised the English 'standard' from which the battle took its name. A curious contraption, it consisted of a ship's mast fixed to a cart. Attached to the mast were the banners of St John of Beverley, St Peter of York, St Wilfred of Ripon and possibly that of St Cuthbert of Durham. While it also served to symbolize the crusading nature of the enterprise, its primary purpose was to act as a rallying point for the English army.

Detailed accounts of the troop formations vary, but it is probable that archers formed the English front line, with spearmen directly behind and unmounted knights in the rear. David's army, having marched down from Darlington, was fronted by the wild, lightly armed Galwegians who insisted, despite David's disapproval, on assuming this suicidal position on a point of honour. Prince Henry's cavalry took up position on the right, with the king himself on the left.

Battle commenced with a ferocious Galwegian charge which was halted in its tracks by murderous volleys of English arrows, the Galwegian chieftains, Ulgeric and Dunewald, being among the casualties. Leaderless, the men of Galloway recoiled, falling back on their own lines. As was so often the case in such situations, they found their path of retreat blocked by their own advancing ranks, which led to even greater confusion and panic.

At this point, Prince Henry tried to turn the tide by leading a charge through the English lines. This was met resolutely by the English knights and the prince's modest party soon found itself surrounded. With difficulty, Henry managed to slip away, abandoning his followers to death or capture.

Scotpit Lane – the burial place of many of the slain of the Battle of the Standard, and where bones were still being unearthed seven centuries later.

His abortive offensive did succeed in diverting attention from King David on the Scottish left so that he too was able to make good his escape. In the space of just two hours, with most of the Scots in full flight, the outcome of the battle was beyond doubt. Although there was no vigorous English pursuit, stragglers and wounded Galwegians were shown no mercy. David succeeded in reaching the safety of Carlisle, his son joining him two days later.

According to contemporary estimates, which are usually unreliable, over 10,000 bodies were buried in mass graves on the battlefield. Given that the estimated size of both armies may have been exaggerated, the likely tally of dead can be moderated accordingly. Even so, the crude manoeuvres of the Scottish tribesmen in making wild, senseless charges against heavily armed and well disciplined opponents – 'tactics' which they were still employing at Culloden, 600 years later – often resulted in the most appalling casualty rates. The cost in human life of King David's ambitions, therefore, would have been terrible enough.

# The Aftermath

The immediate outcome of the battle was that Northumbria – at least nominally – remained in English hands. The English army disbanded immediately after the victory, leaving the borders undefended and enabling the Scots to continue to raid at will. Stephen, whose troubles increased daily, was keen to secure peace at any price. On 9 April 1139, therefore, he signed a treaty with King David, by which Prince Henry was, after all, granted the Earldom of Northumbria. In return, David pledged to support Stephen in his struggle with the rebels in the south – a promise he broke as soon as an opportunity presented itself. Stephen's handling of the Northumbrian question amply demonstrates the weakness of character which lost him so much support. The veterans of the Battle of the Standard must have been less than satisfied with the terms of the Anglo-Scottish pact by which Northumbria was negotiated away in return for worthless guarantees.

In the autumn of 1139, Matilda mounted an invasion. The dastardly Baldwin de Redvers landed in the West Country and occupied Corfe Castle, creating a diversion which enabled Matilda and Robert of Gloucester to land in the east. Stephen hastened to Arundel Castle, where Matilda had taken up her abode but, instead of securing her person, he actually granted her safe passage to join Earl Robert who was canvassing for support in Bristol. This extraordinary decision plunged England into the deplorable state of anarchy for which Stephen's reign is remembered.

This was a time when opportunist barons founded local tyrannies, selling their loyalties first to the royal party and then to Matilda. It was a time of famine, when harvests rotted in the fields, when castles were built by slave labour, and when towns were plundered indiscriminately. It was a time.when the West Country was transformed into a wasteland of deserted settlements and abandoned farms, in a reign of terror redolent of the Dark Ages.

One of the most dangerous enemies Stephen had made was Rannulf, Earl of Chester. A powerful magnate, he had strong hereditary claims on territory in Cumbria. Resentful because his interests had been ignored by Stephen in his peace treaty with the Scots, Rannulf threw in his lot with Matilda. Shortly before Christmas 1140 Rannulf and his half-brother, William of Roumare, seized Lincoln Castle. Stephen's dwindling support meant that he had insufficient troops to strike the decisive blow that the situation demanded and, while he wavered before the castle walls, Robert of Gloucester, at the head of a substantial rebel army, arrived to give battle. In a short, sharp encounter, Stephen's Flemish mercenaries proved unequal to their task, and the king was captured. The wretched citizens of Lincoln were massacred.

Stephen was taken to Bristol Castle, where he was confined in chains. Only the citizens of London and Stephen's queen kept his cause alive. Although Matilda was able to take what she considered to be her rightful place as Queen of England, her triumph was destined to be short-lived, for her haughty and disdainful demeanour began to turn the tide once more in the prisoner Stephen's favour. In fact, Stephen's days of captivity were numbered for, in an encounter between loyalists and rebels at Winchester, the Earl of Gloucester was captured. An exchange of prisoners was arranged and Stephen was released.

And so the civil war continued, with wholesale depredations being committed by self-seeking barons in the name of both parties. Not until Stephen's death in 1154 did the civil strife end, with the nation setting aside nineteen years of anarchy to look forward to a new beginning.

# The Walk

**Distance:** 2¼ miles (3.62 km)

Begin at the monument (point A) which stands on the eastern side of the A167 Northallerton–Darlington road (Pathfinder 620 360979). A lay-by facilitates car parking.

Unlike many battlefield monuments, this one is a useful point of

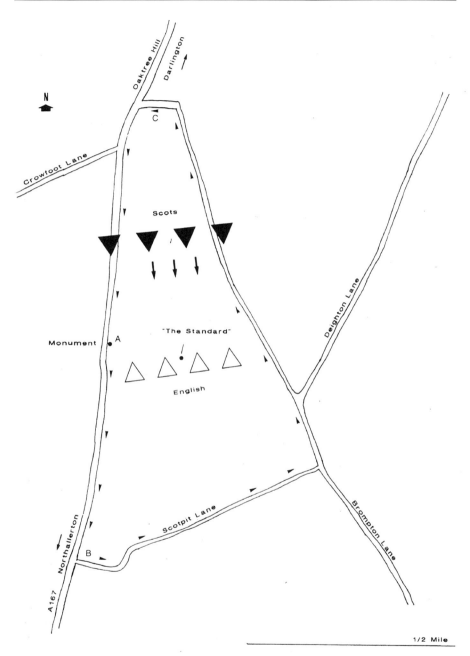

## The Battle of the Standard
## 22 August 1138

reference, marking the centre of the action. The strength of the English position is immediately apparent and one can visualize the front lines strung out across the ridge and down the slope to the road.

Walk south, along the wide grass verge, in the direction of Northallerton. After passing Cinnamire Farm (on the right) look out for a line of trees and bushes running across the field to the left. This marks Scotpit Lane, the area immediately in front of it still being known as The Scot Pits, the mass burial ground of the slaughtered Galwegians – many of whom remained unburied, to be eaten, it was said, by the birds of the air and beasts of the fields.

Turn into Scotpit Lane (point B; Pathfinder 620 359974). A century ago, when Leadman and Barrett wrote about the Battle of the Standard, the lane – connecting the A167 with Brompton Lane – was gated, grassy and still readily passable. Now overgrown, it is barely recognizable as more than a rough path beaten through the undergrowth. For some distance of its half-mile length from the point of entry, it remains quite walkable, but towards the Brompton Lane end, particularly during the summer months, the going becomes quite heavy. In common with many such areas on English battlefields, it is a lonely, cheerless spot.

Emerging on to Brompton Lane, opposite the cottage, turn to the left, to walk up to Oaktree Hill. Again, note the high ground now occupied by Standard Hill Farm (Pathfinder 620 363978), where the English Standard was raised. Continue on up to Oaktree Hill. (On the left is a second Standard Hill Farm!) At Oaktree Hill (point C), Brompton Lane turns sharply to the left before joining the Darlington road. The Scottish position also was strong but, as in many instances in the saga of Anglo-Scottish warfare, the Scots chose to abandon it, to charge downhill and then up to the ridge occupied by the English.

Turn back on to the A167, walk past the garage at the top of the hill and along the nearside verge, back down to the monument.

# Further Explorations

Disastrous as Stephen's reign may have been in social, political and economic terms, in one respect, at least, the period witnessed substantial growth. The Monastic Revival began under Henry I, and the years 1135–54 saw the establishment of more than 100 new foundations. Rievaulx Abbey, the first of the eight great Cistercian houses of Yorkshire, was founded in 1131 by Walter L'Espec, while Fountains Abbey originated in 1132 on land donated by Archbishop Thurstan. Both Thurstan and L'Espec, it will be

The Battlefield Monument, Northallerton.
The monument, commemorating 'Battle
of the Standard AD 1138', stands 2 miles
to the north of Northallerton on the A167.
In the background is Standard Hill Farm,
indicating the English position.

remembered, were prominent in organizing English resistance to the
Scottish invasion leading up to the Battle of the Standard.

One of the lesser known monastic ruins is Mount Grace Priory, a
Carthusian house just 5 miles to the north-east of Northallerton (Landranger
99 4598). Founded at a comparatively late date, in 1398, it is the sole
surviving example of its kind in the country. Even by monastic standards,
the Carthusians endured austere lives, working and studying alone. Food
was served to each monk through a hatch situated by his cell door – the
opening being constructed in such a way as to prohibit any human contact.
The members of the community dined together only on Sundays and
during the great festivals. On all other days, they lived as hermits. Mount
Grace was sponsored by Thomas Holland whom, as Duke of Surrey, was
executed by Henry IV. His remains are believed to have been interred in the
well preserved Priory church, although no trace of his grave has ever been
discovered.

Catterick (Landranger 99 2397), 8 miles to the north-west of
Northallerton, was a military camp 2,000 years ago and it is a military camp
today. Roman Cataractonium stood to the north of present-day Catterick
(Pathfinder 620 228991), commanding Dere Street, an important route
linking York with Hadrian's Wall. When the Romans left, Catterick retained

its importance as a Saxon settlement. The Normans also left their mark on the area, building a castle to the south (Pathfinder 620 254971). This is just one of many instances in which a particular area has retained military significance throughout the ages.

RAF Leeming lies 4 miles to the south-west of Northallerton (Landranger 99 3088). Still in use as a training station, Leeming functioned during the Second World War as a home for bomber squadrons, first with Whitley aircraft and then with the Halifax. No. 10 Squadron, based at Leeming until 1942, saw service on the first Thousand Bomber raid on Cologne, with detachments also taking part in the assaults on the German warships *Scharnhorst* and *Tirpitz*. In August 1942 Canadian squadrons took up residence and remained until the end of hostilities. There were many fatalities on site and in the immediate locality, when disabled bombers returning from missions were unable to effect a successful landing. Perhaps this would account for the sightings of ghostly figures in full flying kit which have been recorded both on the airfield and in its buildings over the years.

Northallerton itself flourished as a coaching town, although the Romans had a settlement here and it is said that William the Conqueror built a fortress, the moat and earthworks of which have been identified (Pathfinder 620 365939). Five hundred years after the Battle of the Standard, on 15 April 1644, Northallerton was again the scene of a fight between the English and a Scottish army of invasion. On this occasion, the Scots, commanded by the Earl of Leven and fighting as allies of the English Parliament, swept aside a single Royalist infantry regiment on its cautious march south.

# Further Information

Useful accounts of the battles are to be found in Leadman's *Battles Fought in Yorkshire* and in Burne's *More Battlefields of England*.

Ordnance Survey maps for the area are Landranger 99 and Pathfinder 620.

The battlefield lies on the A167 Northallerton–Darlington road, about 3 miles to the north of Northallerton itself. Only 5 miles eastward of the A1, the battlefield is readily accessible by road.

Northallerton has retained its railway facility, with a station on the Liverpool–Newcastle and York–Newcastle lines. (Tel: 01904 653022 or 01325 355111 for Northallerton.) There is no National Express coach facility, but for details of local bus links between railway station and battlefield site, call 01609 780780.

At 2¼ miles this is a short walk, but an important one, nevertheless, with unobstructed views of the site of a colourful battle which took place nearly 900 years ago. The circular route is made possible by the continued existence of Scotpit Lane, and it is with some concern that one must note the omission of this feature from the latest (1990) Ordnance Survey Landranger map.

In view of the fact that the walk is a short one, the lack of refreshment facilities should not prove a serious handicap.

# 3
# THE BATTLE OF BOROUGHBRIDGE
## 16 March 1322

## *Introduction*

The start of a new reign is a time of hope. It is a time when the trials and tribulations of the past can be forgotten and when men and women invariably look forward to the future with the confidence that they are embarking on a voyage into a 'golden age' of opportunity, of peace and plenty. This spirit was never more keenly felt than on the accession of Edward II in July 1307.

Edward I ended his life a shadow of his former self. His reform of English law had earned him the title of 'the Lawgiver', but by 1307 his capabilities in this respect had deteriorated to the extent that he prohibited the use of coal, because of its noxious fumes, and prescribed the death penalty for offenders – an act which even the most ardent of twentieth-century environmentalists would consider a trifle excessive.

The new king's financial position was unfortunate in that, owing to his father's prolonged campaigns against France, Wales and Scotland, he inherited a national debt of £200,000. By abandoning the Scottish campaign, Edward made savings although simultaneously offending the northern barons whose lands came under threat. Even so, he had strong family ties with the two most powerful barons in the country – Earl Thomas of Lancaster and Earl Gilbert of Gloucester – a good foundation on which to build.

Edward relinquished much initial goodwill through his infatuation with his male lover, Piers Gaveston. Banished by an outraged Edward I, Gaveston now returned to have the Earldom of Cornwall lavished upon him. The court became a refuge for worthless sycophants and sundry hangers-on, depriving the king of the sound counsel of which he was so sorely in need. Very soon, a strong anti-Gaveston lobby developed in the baronial ranks, culminating in the favourite's execution. Ensconced in

Scarborough Castle for safety, he was lured out by his enemies and beheaded on the orders of the Earl of Warwick.

On the surface, Edward seemed not too perturbed by this development. After all, there were to be found in court circles other attractive young men only too anxious to take Gaveston's place – in particular, one Hugh Despenser, who was to rise to a position of influence which outstripped even the heights attained by his predecessor.

Relations between Edward and the barons were further strained by the inevitable surfacing of old rivalries, revolving around baronial desires to limit the power of the monarchy and the king's wishes to retain and exercise the Royal prerogative. An uneasy peace prevailed, with both sides making concessions, until 1314 when the aggression of Robert the Bruce forced an Anglo-Scottish confrontation culminating in the unmitigated English disaster of Bannockburn.

In addition to the blow to his prestige, Edward's position had also been weakened with the death in battle of the moderate Earl of Gloucester, which left the Earl of Lancaster – who had refused to take part in the Bannockburn campaign – in a dominant position. Relations between Edward and Lancaster gradually became more strained, each vying with the other in attempts to amass armed support. The final break came about as a result of the ambitions of the new Royal favourite, Hugh Despenser, who had acquired a generous share of the deceased Gloucester's estates in Wales. The Lords Marchers, guardians of the frontiers or marches between England and Wales, had helped themselves to much of southern Wales – although the wilder country to the north retained its independence. Lancaster solicited the support of these powerful barons, including the Mortimers, Cliffords, Audleys and the Earl of Hereford, whose own holdings were threatened by Despenser's greed, thereby sparking off a short but bloody civil war.

# The Road to Boroughbridge

The Marchers needed little encouragement to seize Despenser's Welsh acquisitions. In view of the strength of the alliance, as exemplified in this display of muscle, Edward had to agree to his favourite's exile. Having thus secured a breathing space, he was able to plot the piecemeal destruction of his enemies – beginning with Bartholomew Badlesmere, an important landowner and steward of the Royal household. Badlesmere had been courted by the rebel barons and in October 1321, while he was in conference with them at Oxford, Edward besieged his home – Leeds Castle in Kent. The castle fell on 23 October and the garrison was summarily executed. Badlesmere's wife and family were incarcerated in the Tower of London. The Marchers had made no effort to lift the siege, partly because Lancaster seems to have entertained an intense dislike of Badlesmere. Lancaster had also made little effort to cultivate the powerful northern barons, such as Pembroke and Richmond and it was they who had invested Leeds Castle for the king.

This victory gave Edward the confidence to recall Despenser, who had been passing the time by indulging in a little piracy in the English Channel. On 8 December, the same day on which Despenser's exile was revoked, Edward set out for Cirencester on the next stage of his crusade. Here, he received the submission of the first Marcher Lord to capitulate, John Hastings, the Lord of Abergavenny. After Christmas, the Royal army marched north to seize Berkeley Castle while the Welsh, who had been cunningly mobilized to challenge the remaining Marcher strongholds, succeeded in severing communications between the Lords and their fortresses.

On 22 January, at Shrewsbury, the Mortimers submitted to Royal authority, and joined the growing number of penitents in the Tower. Shortly afterwards, Maurice Berkeley and Hugh Audley the Elder surrendered. When it was learned that they had been imprisoned in Wallingford Castle, Audley the Younger, in company with the Earl of Hereford and Sir Roger D'Amory, fled to join Lancaster.

Although his plans were proceeding smoothly, Edward was still concerned about the possible extent of rebel support. As levies were not flocking to the Royal banner as eagerly as he had hoped, he was forced to delay his final move against Lancaster until early in March, when he moved out from Coventry. The rebels, meanwhile, were marching down from Doncaster, their leader aware of the fact that, due to his own inactivity, his strong hand had been outplayed.

At Burton-on-Trent, the opposing forces met for the first time. Lancaster had already lost irreplaceable stores while trying to ford a flooded stream, but now the swollen River Trent worked in his favour as he was able to hold the bridge separating the two armies for three days. When Edward effected a crossing further upstream, the rebels, having senselessly set fire to the town, advanced to give battle. However, discouraged by the size of Edward's force, they retreated northwards. In so doing, Lancaster hoped to buy time to gather more support. In particular, he expected aid from Scotland and additional troops from a recruitment campaign undertaken by a friend, Robert Holland. The latter expectation came to naught when Holland, who interpreted the withdrawal as a sign of defeat, surrendered his 500 men to the king at Derby – a sentiment echoed by the garrisons at Tutbury and Kenilworth, both of which threw in the towel. As Lancaster's manpower dwindled, so Edward's increased, and it must have been a particularly gratifying experience for the king when he was joined at Lichfield by Despenser with more men.

Lancaster managed to stay ahead of the Royal forces, which kept up a hot pursuit under the command of the Earls of Surrey and Kent. At length, he gained the security of his own castle at Pontefract, which he thought capable of withstanding a protracted siege, but the remnants of his supporters – in particular, Sir Roger Clifford – insisted on going further north, to make a stand at the impregnable Dunstanburgh Castle in Northumberland. Bowing to this pressure, the disheartened Lancaster set out for Dunstanburgh on a route which took the rebels via Boroughbridge, where they arrived on 16 March 1322, in the hope of resting safely overnight.

# The Battle of Boroughbridge

Lancaster's scouting arrangements must have left much to be desired for, after his army had begun to settle in, he learned that the bridge over the Ure, at the north end of the town, was already in Royalist hands. This had come about through the intervention of the Warden of Carlisle and the Western Marches, Sir Andrew de Harcla, who had been instructed to muster northern forces on behalf of the king. De Harcla had been en route to join the Earls of Surrey and Kent when, learning of Lancaster's progress towards Boroughbridge, he had made a detour in an attempt to reach the town ahead of him.

Faced with the dread prospect of being caught between de Harcla and the main Royal army advancing from the south, the rebels were compelled to try to take the bridge. Prior to doing so, Lancaster attempted to parley with de Harcla, reminding him of past favours – de Harcla had received his knighthood from the earl – and promising him further advancement if he threw in his lot with the rebels. But de Harcla would have none of it. Although his own force would have been numerically inferior to Lancaster's, he also knew that the bridge would not be an easy objective. A narrow, rickety wooden structure, the bridge spanned 60 yards of water and one suspects that the heavier daily traffic used the ford further downstream, at Milby. And de Harcla had deployed his men well, knights and men-at-arms before the bridge, with archers on the higher ground to the rear.

When it was clear that de Harcla could not be won over, battle commenced. At first, the contest was limited to volleys of arrows which the archers of each side projected across the river. While this may have suited de Harcla, the rebel barons could not afford to allow themselves to be pinned down. In an effort to break the deadlock, therefore, the Earl of Hereford led a charge on to the bridge, while Lancaster, commanding a party of horse, tried to outflank the Royalists by crossing at the ford.

Boroughbridge, from the north bank of the River Ure. The present-day stone bridge occupies the site of the fourteenth-century wooden structure which was the objective of the Earl of Lancaster's rebel army. Down through the centuries, remnants of arms and armour have been found below the bridge.

To Lancaster's dismay, he arrived at the ford to find it well defended by more archers who resisted all his attempts to cross over and, after suffering heavy losses, he was forced to retire. At the bridge, Hereford made good progress before meeting his end at the hands of a Welsh spearman who, having climbed beneath the bridge, disembowelled the fearless earl with an upward thrust of his spear. Perhaps this episode, as recounted by contemporary chroniclers, owes something to the account of the courageous Norwegian's death at Stamford Bridge (see p. 6) but, whatever the cause of Hereford's demise, it had the effect of spreading panic among the rebel ranks. When Roger Clifford was felled by an arrow, the offensive broke down completely, the rebels withdrawing in disorder.

Cognisant of the fact that the fight was lost, Lancaster concluded a temporary truce with de Harcla, by which he agreed to surrender on the following day or suffer the consequences. This led to the extraordinary situation of the vanquished retiring into Boroughbridge to sleep soundly while the victors had to remain vigilant throughout the night, continuing to guard both the bridge and the ford.

It may have been that de Harcla, mindful of his debt to Lancaster, wanted to give him an opportunity to slip away and that he intended to explain his behaviour in terms of adherence to chivalric principles. In any event, the dawn saw the arrival of Sir Simon Ward, High Sheriff of Yorkshire, with Royalist reinforcements and, to avoid accusations of collusion with the rebels, de Harcla had to launch an assault on the town. Abandoned by all save a faithful few, Lancaster fled to claim sanctuary in the chapel in the Market Square. Dragged from the altar, he was stripped of his armour and, compelled to wear his servant's clothing, was shipped to York where he was pelted with mud by the citizens – the same folk who would gladly have adorned him with garlands, had his revolt been successful.

# The Aftermath

In his *Guide to the Battlefields of Britain and Ireland*, Lt Col Howard Green remarks that no battle on British soil made less impact on British history than Boroughbridge. In fact, the political repercussions were considerable.

Lancaster himself was tried at Pontefract and condemned as a traitor. The man who had inherited five earldoms was taunted by the mob as he was led to his death – a relatively merciful one as he was beheaded instead of suffering the traitor's customary punishment of being hanged, drawn and quartered. Having thus disposed of his main adversary, Edward embarked on a pogrom of revenge against all his opponents. Those who were unable to escape into exile were slaughtered or imprisoned, and for years afterwards, the remains of those executed hung in chains as a deterrent to all who would challenge Royal authority. All the political concessions which the barons had been able to prise out of the king were annulled and Hugh Despenser was free to amass a personal fortune of a magnitude which almost defies description.

As Edward occupied himself with butchering his enemies, strange events were taking place at Pontefract. Lancaster's remains had been interred in the Priory Church by the monks of Pontefract, and his tomb became the resort of pilgrims. Miracles were performed – the dead were raised, sight was restored to the blind and lunatics regained their reason. In much the same way that another rebel earl – Simon de Montfort – had taken on the mantle of martyr sixty years before, Thomas, Earl of Lancaster became a candidate for canonization, and the wave of veneration for this hitherto universally reviled individual was such that the government was compelled to take measures to discourage acts of adoration.

Another curious incident involved Sir Andrew de Harcla. In his extremity,

Lancaster had cursed his former protégé, foretelling for him a shameful traitor's death 'within the year'. This seemed most unlikely when, following the Battle of Boroughbridge, de Harcla was created Earl of Carlisle. However, on 14 October 1322 an English army raised by Edward to counter continuing Scottish depredations in the north was surprised and destroyed by the Scots at Byland Abbey (Landranger 100 5478). Edward was compelled to flee for his life and much of his treasure, including the crown jewels, fell into Scottish hands. De Harcla, with upwards of 20,000 men at his command, had failed to arrive – according to some, he had deliberately held back – and he was made the scapegoat for the disaster, which had left the Scots free to run riot as far south as present-day Humberside. Found guilty of collusion with the Scots, he was hanged, drawn and beheaded on 3 March 1323. Thus, 'within the year', Lancaster's prophecy was fulfilled.

During his flight, Edward had abandoned Queen Isabella and the already strained relations between the two led to the king's downfall. When war with France broke out in 1324, Isabella, accompanied by the heir to the throne, Prince Edward, was sent as an emissary to discuss peace terms with the French king, Charles IV, who was also her brother. Once safely across the Channel, she began to plot with the English exiles – in particular with Roger Mortimer. Condemned to death, Mortimer had escaped from the Tower. Now he took revenge on Edward by becoming the queen's lover. In September 1326, at the head of an invasion force, Isabella and Mortimer landed in Suffolk. As a result of his excesses since the triumph at Boroughbridge, Edward's support wilted. Both he and Hugh Despenser were captured by Henry of Lancaster – Thomas's brother – in Wales, where they had sought refuge. Despenser was executed at Hereford while Edward, forced to abdicate in favour of his son, was imprisoned, first at Kenilworth and then in Berkeley Castle. His fate remains a mystery. Some said that he was brutally put to death. Others maintained that he escaped to live out his days as a hermit in Cologne, with an opportunity to reflect upon the error of his ways in failing to keep his friends close and his enemies even closer.

# The Walk

**Distance:** 4 miles (6.44 km)

Begin by the bridge itself. On the north bank of the Ure, a picnic area (point A; Pathfinder 653 395672) is accessible from the roundabout. This spot provides one with a good view of the present-day bridge from upstream.

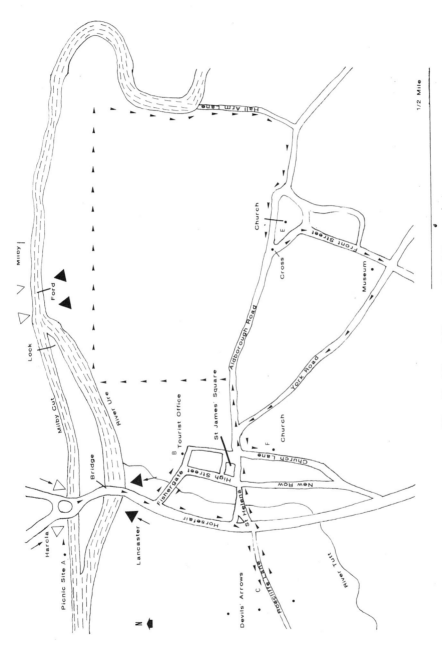

**The Battle of Boroughbridge
16 March 1322**

1/2 Mile

N

The land on this side of the river has a gentle rise overlooking the opposite bank, providing a good vantage point for de Harcla's archers.

Cross over the bridge into Horsefair. A short detour into Fishergate on the left facilitates a visit to the Tourist Information Centre (point B). Turn back into Horsefair and continue down to Bar Lane, on the right. At the end of the lane, just before the A1 overpass, can be found the Devil's Arrows (point C), three standing stones of millstone grit. Two stand in the field to the right, and one is hidden among the trees to the left. Three thousand years ago they were hauled laboriously – each weighs 30 tons – from Knaresborough, a distance of 6½ miles. Originally, there were four, standing on a north–south axis, but the fourth was torn down and used to build a bridge over the River Tutt – the Ure's tributary running through the town. They may have played a role in fertility rites but, whatever their purpose, one cannot help wondering what effect their presence would have had upon the superstitious minds of the combatants.

Walk back up to Horsefair, bearing left and then right into St Helena, which leads on to Aldborough Road. Opposite the school is a public footpath leading down to the Ure. This links up with a raised riverside path which follows the south bank of the Ure. Lancaster would have crossed these open fields to reach the ford at Milby (point D; Pathfinder 654 402675), which lies beyond the lock. As at the bridge, the north bank commands a clear view of the land to the south, which helped de Harcla's archers keep the rebels at bay. Continue along the path to Hall Arm Lane which runs down by the side of Aldborough Hall into Aldborough.

Aldborough, once of much greater importance than Boroughbridge, was originally called Iseur. As the flourishing Brigante tribal capital, under the Roman occupation, it became Isurium Brigantum. Although fragments of the Roman defensive walls and two tessellated pavements may be seen, on a site managed by English Heritage, much work remains to be done.

Turn right into the village and walk up to St Andrew's Church (point E) dating from the fourteenth century. Stone from the Roman buildings was used in the construction of the church tower and the church itself contains a statue of the Roman god Mercury – a curious home for a symbol of paganism. A shade further along the Aldborough road is the restored battle cross (Pathfinder 654 405665). Also fourteenth century in origin, it stood in the market-place in Boroughbridge until 1852, when it was removed to its present site.

Turn into Front Street – the main street of the Roman settlement – and walk down towards the National Heritage site and Roman Museum.

Walk down to the crossroads and turn to the right, into York Road, which leads back into Boroughbridge. On reaching the old town, take a left turn into Church Lane, to see St James's Church (point F). The chapel in which Lancaster sought sanctuary stood in St James's Square, although fragments

The Battle Cross. Commemorating the Battle of Boroughbridge, the cross stood in the market-place for five hundred years. In 1852 it was removed to its present resting place in Aldborough.

of carved stone belonging to the chapel were built into the walls of the present-day church.

St James's Square is certainly a fitting site for a church, which was pulled down to facilitate the exploitation of an artesian well beneath it. Walk back past the square and on into the town, where one may take refreshment at any one of the town's excellent inns before making one's way back to the starting-point at the picnic site.

## *Further Explorations*

Three miles to the east of Boroughbridge – as the crow flies – is the village of Myton-on-Swale. The relevant OS Pathfinder 654 depicts another, little known, battle site – that of White Battle (432668). After Bannockburn, the Scots pillaged the north of England at will. In 1318 they penetrated as far south as Pontefract. A year later, another foray was met by armed resistance organized by one of Edward II's more able ministers, William Melton, Archbishop of Canterbury. Melton's army, which included monks and clergymen, proved a poor match for the Scots, and soon took to its heels. In fact, this particular raid was a tactical one. The Scots had taken the town of Berwick and the Yorkshire foray was designed to divert the attention of a large English army which had been mustered to win back this important military and administrative centre. The stratagem worked and the English abandoned their siege.

After putting Melton's army to flight, the invaders went on to pillage much of Wharfedale. The effects of raids such as this were devastating, with the religious houses of the Yorkshire Dales often bearing the brunt of the Gaelic onslaughts. Local communities often depended for their survival upon the sound economic management of an abbey or priory, the wholesale destruction of crops, livestock and buildings often leading to famine and destitution.

Knaresborough lies 6 miles to the south of Boroughbridge on the Harrogate road, and is the site of one of the great Yorkshire castles (Landranger 104 3456). Of the original Knaresborough Castle, founded after the Conquest by Serlo de Burgh, no trace remains. The present ruins are all that is left of the castle as rebuilt in the first half of the fourteenth century. The murderers of Thomas Becket were given refuge here and Richard II was held prisoner within the castle walls before his removal to Pontefract. Occupying an excellent defensive position, with a precipitous fall to the river on one side and a deep moat on the other, the Royalist-held castle withstood a siege for six weeks during the Civil War, finally surrendering to Fairfax on 20 December 1644. Four years later, it was rendered harmless by being dismantled on the orders of Parliament.

Knaresborough is closely associated with the ardently Royalist Slingsby family. Sir Henry Slingsby, whose diaries constitute valuable primary source material, survived both Naseby and Marston Moor, only for a Parliamentary tribunal to relieve him of his head on Tower Hill in 1658. Still preserved in Knaresborough Castle is a suit of armour believed to have been worn by Sir Henry at Marston Moor. His tomb, along with those of several others of the family, may be seen in the church (Landranger 104 3556.) The stone of the church tower looks as if it has been burnt. During the Scottish invasion of 1381 Knaresborough was sacked and the Scots, finding that the inhabitants had taken refuge in the church tower, piled up straw and timber around it in an attempt to burn them out.

Like Northallerton, Boroughbridge is a coaching town which has seen far busier days. The only reminders of its golden age, when horse-drawn traffic rattled to London and Scotland at speeds of anything up to 10 mph, are the substantial Dickensian coaching inns. Although its situation on the Great North Road has been devalued with the provision of a by-pass, along which horseless carriages now thunder at 90 mph, Boroughbridge remains an excellent touring centre for the Yorkshire Dales – just as Northallerton benefits from its position in respect of the North Yorkshire Moors.

# Further Information

The Battle of Boroughbridge has not attracted a great deal of attention from historians. One of the best accounts is to be found in Leadman's *Battles Fought in Yorkshire*.

Ordnance Survey Landranger 99 covers the area, but this is one of those instances in which two Pathfinder maps are needed: Pathfinder 653 for Boroughbridge and Pathfinder 654 for Aldborough.

The position of Boroughbridge on the A1 makes it easy to locate. At one time, the Great North Road ran through the town, but a by-pass has long since replaced the old road running over the bridge. Even so, continuous heavy traffic, coupled with perpetual roadworks on the A1 means that motorists must plan for often long delays. Parking facilities in the town are adequate. If the Monday market is avoided, parking can be found in Back Lane, in addition to the picnic site recommended as a starting-point for the walk.

Boroughbridge is served by British Rail at Ripon and York (tel: 01904 642155). For details of connecting bus services, call 01609 780780. It is a sign of the times that despite its historic importance as a coaching town, the Boroughbridge of today has no National Express coach service.

The area in the vicinity of the bridge and that adjacent to the riverside walks to Milby and beyond would not, at the time of writing (1994), appear to be in much danger from development, although the upgrading of the A1 by-pass has led to applications for planning permission to build a motorway service area to the south-west, between Boroughbridge and Minskip. Similarly, with no immediate threat to the Roman remains at Aldborough, there has been no necessity to press ahead with excavations. Should the situation change, one fears that the painstaking work involved would have to be undertaken within far too limited a time-scale. The museum is open during the summer season only. For details call 01423 322768.

# 4
# THE BATTLE OF NEVILLE'S CROSS
## 17 October 1346

## *Introduction*

The year 1346 witnessed two international battles in which the English were involved. Both resulted in decisive English victories, and neither led to any permanent cessation of hostilities between the protagonists. This is not too surprising because the English, although they were very good at winning battles, always proved unable to capitalize on their victories – a tradition which continues to the present day. The second of these battles would not have been fought at all if the outcome of the first had been different. The latter was fought on 26 August 1346 on the banks of the Somme, at Crécy.

Crécy was the first of the three famous medieval English victories over the French, all of them – Crécy, Poitiers (1356) and Agincourt (1415) – demonstrating the supremacy of the English longbow. Leaving aside the English naval victory at Sluys in 1340, Crécy was also the first major battle of what came to be known as the Hundred Years' War between England and France, a conflict which developed out of the demise of Charles IV of France, who died without leaving an heir. Although Philip of Valois took the throne, the English king, Edward III, decided to exercise his own claim, through his mother, Isabella, to the title.

Also central to hostilities was the problem of the Duchy of Gascony, worth in excess of £13,000 per annum to its landlord. It was also the last remaining major foothold which the English had in France. Philip wanted to acquire it and Edward wished to retain it. In 1337 Philip took Gascony, thus starting a war which was to continue, on and off, for over a century, finally drawing to a close in 1453 with the French victory at Chatillon.

Perhaps because he had drawn up an invasion plan as early as 1329, Edward's response to the French seizure of Gascony was swift. Having forged what was to become a financially crippling alliance with the German Emperor, Ludwig IV, the English king was able to advance into French territory at the head of an allied army in 1339. The campaign did not go well and was followed by six years of abortive raids and fitful attempts to find a diplomatic solution.

At length, in 1346, following English successes in the field, engineered by the Earl of Lancaster, Edward mounted a further major offensive. Counting on the elements of speed and surprise, he attacked – and took – Caen. Pressing on inland, the victors found themselves pursued by a numerically superior French army. At Crécy, taking up a strong defensive position, they stood their ground. The French, relying on the tragically magnificent cavalry charges of their nobility, were routed. Factors responsible for the English success included Edward's generalship and his effective use of his men-at-arms and archers.

The English moved off to lay siege to Calais, which Edward coveted as a base for military operations and as a port for English goods. The French, meanwhile, retired to lick their wounds and to seek ways of relieving English pressure in order to give them time to regroup. One avenue to be explored in this connection concerned the Scots, who could always be depended upon to render assistance when required.

As Edward's continental interests commanded more of his time and attention, so English efforts to keep the Scots at bay lapsed. Scotland had been governed by Edward Balliol, an English collaborator, while David II, heir to Robert the Bruce, was consigned to exile in France. In 1341 David had made a triumphant return home and now, in 1346, was keen to repay French hospitality by invading England at the request of Philip. Thus, the French defeat at Crécy paved the way for the second historic English military engagement of 1346: the Battle of Neville's Cross.

# The Road to Neville's Cross

The English were acutely aware of the potential threat to the security of the nation, should France and Scotland mount a combined invasion. Capable of putting a combined army of perhaps 40,000 men in the field, the two countries might well swamp the relatively small army which any English king was able to muster at any given time. In the present instance, although the French were temporarily *hors de combat*, Edward was tied down at Calais, and the Scots must have felt that, in planning a late-summer offensive, the absence of the master tactician would give them an edge.

The size of the Scottish army is unknown, but estimates of 30,000 are exaggerated. A figure of 15,000 would, perhaps, be nearer the mark. The force, with King David at its head, crossed the border at Carlisle, laying

The capture of David II at the Battle of Neville's Cross. While contemporary paintings depicting battle scenes pay scant regard to scale and perspective, they do portray the horror and confusion of medieval warfare. Here, the wounded Scottish monarch, taken prisoner by John Copeland, is about to embark on a lengthy period of captivity. In fact, the conditions of his detention were so comfortable that, upon his return to Scotland eleven years later, he pined for the English luxuries he was no longer able to enjoy. (Bibliothèque Nationale, Paris)

waste everything in its path. Lanercost Priory was plundered, as was Hexham Abbey. Continuing via Corbridge, the Scots appeared to be aiming for Durham – in fact, they camped just 2 miles to the west of the city, at Bearpark.

It is not clear whether David had any intention of attempting to take Durham. The citizens and the monks of the Cathedral were terror-stricken at the prospect, but although the Scots would have been difficult to dislodge once in possession of the city, it would have proved a tough nut to crack. It seems, instead, that the Scots were content to use Bearpark as a base for raiding the surrounding countryside, and their ultimate purpose may well have been to lure what they hoped and expected would be an inferior English army into a trap.

The scenario was not dissimilar to that which had culminated in the Battle of the Standard 200 years before or, indeed, to the situation which would lead to the Battle of Otterburn in 1388. In each case, the Scots took advantage of the English king's preoccupation with other matters, and in each case responsibility for the defence of the realm devolved upon the powerful northern barons.

In the present instance, the man at the helm should have been the Bishop of Durham, Thomas Hatfield. However, he had accompanied Edward to France and it fell to the Archbishop of York, William Zouche, to coordinate the resistance. Those who answered the call included representatives of the two great rival families which bore the brunt of border warfare – Henry Percy and Ralph Neville. With remarkable speed and efficiency, the English force was assembled at Bishop Auckland. Although it is often claimed that it was far inferior numerically to that of the Scots, the armies may have been fairly evenly matched.

From Bishop Auckland, Neville moved out to Kirk Merrington and from there to Ferry Hill where the English surprised Sir William Douglas and a Scottish raiding party, pursuing them as far as Sunderland Bridge. Douglas managed to escape to carry news of the proximity of the English army to David, who appears to have shown little concern. Douglas advised him to retreat to enable the Scots to select an advantageous battleground – counsel which was contemptuously ignored, David dismissing the English as a horde of 'miserable monks and pig-drivers'.

Not being cognisant of the Scottish master plan – if, indeed, there was one – Neville had been in a quandary as to how to proceed. Should he march to the relief of Durham and risk being bottled up inside its walls, or would it be advisable to seek an early confrontation with the invaders? In the end, it was decided to give battle, and the English advanced northwards from Sunderland Bridge, sweeping to the west of the city to take up a position in the vicinity of Neville's Cross, and in sight of Bearpark, from where the Scots advanced to meet them.

# The Battle of Neville's Cross

Each side assumed three divisions. Ralph Neville faced King David in the centre, the English right under Henry Percy faced Robert, the High Steward, while Sir Thomas Rokeby with the Archbishop of York on the English left wing faced Sir William Douglas.

It was Douglas who made the opening move. As his men, with characteristic impetuosity, charged forward, they found their progress hampered to some extent by a small ravine, and were forced to swerve to their left – into the Scottish centre. The English bowmen, quick to capitalize on the situation, poured destructive volleys of arrows into the congested enemy ranks. Cognisant of the damage being wrought, a Scottish nobleman (named by some sources as William Graham) headed a small, unauthorized cavalry charge into the body of archers and succeeded in scattering them. Robert followed up this piece of individual heroism with a more organized assault on Percy's wing. Once again, the English front line gave way. In the centre, King David's men were more than holding their own.

While the battle raged, something rather curious was happening on the crest of a hill known as Maiden's Bower, to the east of the Scottish position. Here, a number of ecclesiastics from the Cathedral had gathered to pray, the focus of their devotions being a relic – the sacred corporas cloth – of St Cuthbert. Fixed to a spear in order to function as a sacred banner, it was used to send news of the conflict to monks looking out from the Cathedral tower, which could be seen from the hillock. Unmolested by the Scots, the priests remained at their outpost for the three-hour duration of the battle, employing their own semaphore to keep their colleagues within the Cathedral walls informed of progress.

It was beginning to look as though the Scots would carry the day when an English cavalry charge transformed the situation. Robert's infantry was put to flight, leaving the centre dangerously exposed. The combined pressure exerted by Neville pushing forward to their front and de Baliol's cavalry now encroaching on their left flank proved too much for David's division and they, too, wilted, leaving Douglas on the Scottish right to bear the brunt of the English attack – against which he soon gave way.

King David and a human shield of devoted knights fought on until exhaustion forced the survivors to surrender. David himself, badly wounded, was taken prisoner. It is said that he struck his captor, John Copeland, Governor of Roxburgh Castle, in an attempt to goad him into killing him, and so evade the ignominy of imprisonment. According to another, less edifying version of the Scottish king's capture, he slipped away, unwounded,

Durham Cathedral. From the lofty heights of the central tower, ecclesiastics were able to receive news of the battle from colleagues clustered around their standard on Maiden's Bower.

from the battlefield and was found hiding under a bridge spanning the River Browney, to the east of Bearpark.

The slaughter of the vanquished was great. With their customary over-confidence, the Scots had failed to select a battleground which provided an adequate escape route, should everything fail to go according to plan. Thus, the terrain which had hampered their advance now seriously compromised their withdrawal. The constrictions of the ravine and the River Browney to their right, and the marsh to their left made them an easy mass target for their pursuers. Many of the slain were men of note. On the English side, however, the only person of rank to lose his life was Randolph, Lord Hastings.

# The Aftermath

King David remained, for a time, in the custody of his captor, Copeland. Edward III's queen, Philippa, asked for David to be surrendered to her, but Copeland refused, on the grounds that he felt justified in handing over his prisoner only to the English king in person. Hearing of this, Edward (who was at Calais) sent for his loyal subject, knighted him and granted him a pension to the extent of five hundred pounds per annum, with a request that he obey the queen. Copeland complied although, secretly, he may have considered his annuity trifling compared with the huge ransom which his prisoner was worth.

While in Copeland's care, David had been kept securely under lock and key. When he passed into Royal ownership, although he was despatched to the Tower, his conditions of imprisonment were not particularly onerous, and it is said that during the eleven years of captivity which followed, he acquired a taste for such comforts of life as were missing in the harsher environment north of the Border.

Facing a leaderless enemy, Edward might have been expected to capitalize on the English victory at Neville's Cross by bringing the Scots to heel. That this was not accomplished is usually attributed to the ravages of the Black Death, introduced to the British Isles via the Dorset port of Weymouth in 1348. Despite efforts to limit the spread of this horrific disease, it soon covered the entire country. At first, the Scots rejoiced, but when it reached the Highlands, they realized that this was no punishment divinely inflicted upon the English alone.

Estimates of the plague's death toll during the later fourteenth century vary. Perhaps as much as half of the total population (standing at around four million) of the British Isles was wiped out. More cautious – perhaps, over-cautious – historians argue that a normally high death rate was simply accelerated, and that this was by no means a social and economic disaster because, by the standards of the time, Europe was over-populated. Certainly, there was no shortage of men to fight battles. Although no major battle took place on British soil in the forty-two years between 1346 and 1388, border fighting continued and in 1352, Edward was able to muster sufficient men to mount his famous 'Burnt Candlemas' campaign during which he laid waste Scottish territory from the Tweed to the Forth. Perhaps it is significant that this was a winter expedition – a most unusual undertaking at a time when warfare was strictly a fair-weather pastime. During the winter months, outbreaks of plague tended to subside and it may have been for this reason that Edward was compelled to break with tradition. However, the wars with the French did continue, and such were the reserves of manpower that it was possible to assemble an army for the Black Prince to lead to victory at Poitiers in September 1356.

Thanks to his position in the comparative isolation of the Tower of London, King David survived the Black Death. In his absence, Robert the Steward took on the job of ruling Scotland in his place. His task has been described as a thankless one, but he made no Herculean efforts to free his king, and it seemed as if the haggling over the issue of a fitting ransom would continue indefinitely. In an attempt to bring matters to a successful conclusion, David was not above suggesting that, in exchange for his freedom, arrangements might be made for Edward or one of his sons to inherit the Scottish throne. According to one story, David was released from his confinement in 1352, on the understanding that he would return of his own free will, in order to try to persuade Robert and the Scottish parliament to accept this compromise.

In the end, however, a purely financial agreement was reached. In return for their monarch's freedom, the Scots agreed to pay one hundred thousand marks, payable in interest-free instalments of ten thousand marks over ten years.

And so, after eleven years in the hands of his enemies, King David returned home to his people with whom he had, in his absence, grown sadly out of touch. Only a small proportion of the ransom was ever paid. Perhaps Copeland's bargain had not, after all, been quite so disadvantageous.

# The Walk

**Distance:** 3½ miles (5.63 km)

Begin at Framwellgate Bridge (point A) on Silver Street (Pathfinder 572 273425). Walking westward, with the castle and Cathedral at one's back, cross the Wear. Over the river, where the road forks, bear right into North

Road. Cross over the roundabout, walking beneath the railway viaduct, before veering left into Sutton Street and then sharp right into Waddington Street. At the end of Waddington Street is a footpath leading up through woods towards Flass Bog. By following this route, one can appreciate the extent to which the terrain hampered the Scottish left wing.

Retracing one's steps, return down Waddington Street and turn right into Sutton Street, sharp right again into Flass Street – and so into Redhills Lane. Walk up Redhills Lane – a very steep climb. (Note Miner's Hall, dating from 1915, on the right, a reminder of the proud past of a vanished industry.) At the top of Redhills Lane, on the right, is a comprehensive school. Just before reaching the running track, encased in the trees is Maiden's Bower (Pathfinder 572 264427), the vantage point utilized by the party from the Cathedral.

Redhills Lane emerges on to the Great North Road (point B). Walk down into Toll House Road, almost opposite. On the right, at the end of the line of houses is a footpath leading up to Arbour House – and beyond to Bearpark, where the Scots camped before the battle. A little further along, on the left, is a track leading down, across the River Browney, to Baxter Wood (Pathfinder 572 255423). By walking down the track (point C), one can see how the terrain restricted the forward movement of the Scottish right wing.

Return to the Great North Road and turn right to walk down towards Neville's Cross. The centre of the English line may well have occupied a position across the A1 at a point where the road crosses over the railway line. At the junction with the A690, turn to the left. Tucked away from the road, by the Working Men's Club (point D), are the remains of a monument erected at the sole expense of Ralph Neville. Vandalized in 1589, the sorry stump is all that has survived of the original, elaborately carved pillar.

Continue along Crossgate. Beyond the church on the right, turn into Archery Rise. At the far end, bear to the left. What looks like a cul-de-sac does, in fact, have a public footpath leading from it. Turn to the right and follow this footpath round to the Observatory (Pathfinder 572 268415) – a useful reference point. The footpath continues past the Observatory, downhill, and through the fields (be prepared to negotiate a stile and gate) to a track servicing Durham School. This track emerges on to Quarryheads. Across the road is a path which leads down to Prebends Bridge, and a recrossing of the Wear. From the bridge, follow the path into South Bailey and on up to the Cathedral (point E).

Like many another cathedral, Durham had humble beginnings. A thousand years ago, a group of refugees from Lindisfarne, seeking a resting place for the remains of St Cuthbert, built a wooden church on this sandstone outcrop. In 1093 a start on the present-day Cathedral was made by William of Calais. Later development, as with other ecclesiastical establishments throughout Northumbria, owed much to the Nevilles. Ralph, the victor of Neville's Cross, was the first layman to be buried in the

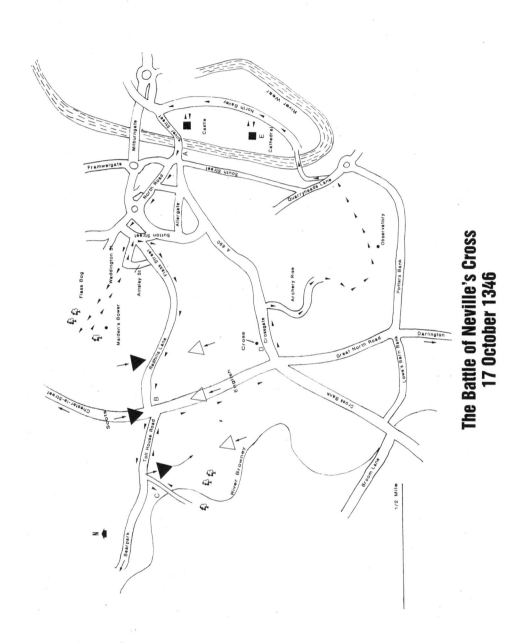

The Battle of Neville's Cross
17 October 1346

Neville's Cross. The original cross – of which but a fragment remains – was said to be over 10 ft in height, with exquisite ornamentation which included the coats-of-arms of the Neville family. It survived until 1589 when 'the same was broken down and defaced by some lewd, contemptuous and wicked persons, thereto encouraged (as it seemed) by some who loved Christ the worse for the Crosse sake, as utterly and spightfully contemning all ancient ceremonies and monuments'.

Cathedral. A lengthy climb leads to the top of the central tower, from where, three and a half centuries ago, the worried monks peered out towards Maiden's Bower.

Leaving the Cathedral, turn left into North Bailey and continue along to the castle. Now belonging to the University of Durham, the castle, in a wellnigh impregnable position, never fell to the Scots. The present structure was begun in 1072 as a fortified residence for the Bishop of Durham, but the military potential of the site had been recognized long before. Indeed, attacks by the Normans themselves had been successfully repulsed by the Saxons with the aid of rudimentary earth and timber fortifications.

Return to North Bailey – which develops into Saddler Street – and walk down into Silver Street to the starting-point. Refreshment in the Coach and Eight on Framwellgate Bridge, overlooking the river, is recommended.

# Further Explorations

With the Cathedral and castle included in the walk, the stranger, with little knowledge of Durham's heritage, may be forgiven for thinking that little of relevant historical interest remains to be seen in the area. However, nothing could be further from the truth.

For example, Bearpark (Pathfinder 572 243438) was the campsite of King David's army before the battle. The favourite residence of Durham's medieval priors, Bearpark suffered much at the hands of the Scots, particularly in 1315 when the estate was ransacked, and then, again, in 1346, when David's men committed further acts of vandalism. The ruins are approached by the footpath via Arbour House and Toll House Road.

To the south of Bearpark is Brancepeth and Brancepeth Castle (Landranger 93 2237), one of the oldest fortified castles in the country. Originally owned by the de Bulmer family (along with Sheriff Hutton – see p. 10), it passed, by marriage, to the Nevilles in the late twelfth century. Oliver Cromwell is said to have lodged here en route to Scotland. The castle was much altered at the turn of the nineteenth century and little of the ancient fabric now remains. Group tours can sometimes be arranged (tel: 0191 378 0628 for details).

Also of interest in Brancepeth is St Brandon's Church (Landranger 93 2237) which owes much to the patronage of the Neville family, commemorated in a number of monuments – in particular, to Robert Neville (killed at Berwick in a border skirmish in 1319) and Ralph Neville (2nd Earl of Westmorland) who actually managed to die a natural death in 1484.

To the north of Durham can be found the remains of Finchale Priory (Pathfinder 572 296471). In the Durham volume of his King's England series, Arthur Mee refers to Finchale as 'the loveliest ruin in the country'. Originally the site of a modest hermitage built by St Godric in 1110, it developed gradually into a holiday retreat for the monks of Durham Cathedral. Traces of St Godric's stone chapel can still be seen. Now in the care of English Heritage, the ruins may be viewed free of charge at any reasonable time.

A little further to the north of Durham is Lumley Castle (Landranger 88 2851). It developed from a manor-house built by Sir Ralph Lumley in the fourteenth century. Once again, much altered in successive centuries, it now functions as a hotel. In 1642 the Royalist Sir Richard Lumley held it for the king, although two years later, the garrison was evacuated peacefully when the Earl of Newcastle abandoned his bases in the area.

A once-proud tower of a medieval manor-house, now reduced to little more than a curiosity, can be found in the village of Ludworth. Ludworth Tower (Pathfinder 572 357414) was built in the mid-fourteenth century. All that now remains is a ruinous wall, perched high on a grassy mound.

Pittington once constituted the property of the Community of St Cuthbert. The Prior's Hall – long since vanished – became yet another summer residence for the Priors of Durham. The site of the ancient hall lies before the Church of St Laurence (Pathfinder 572 328437), itself a building of some importance. Sometimes described as one of the most interesting Saxon churches in the country, it contains the stone monument of a knight, who is believed to have died around 1250, and a stone carved in the shape of two small coffins – thought to represent a thirteenth-century grave cover for twin infants.

As Arthur Mee, once more, remarks in his King's England volume, few counties have a more remarkable history than County Durham, and few are less generally well known and appreciated.

## Further Information

Accounts of the battle are to be found in Barrett's *Battles and Battlefields in England* and in Burne's *More Battlefields of England*.

Ordnance Survey maps for the area are Landranger 88 and Pathfinder 572. A locally purchased street map will prove useful.

By road, Durham is accessible via the A1(M) with city centre parking available in the Cathedral multi-storey car park. (Care should be taken when using the multi-storey as manoeuvrability is very limited.)

For details of British Rail services to Durham, call 0191 232 6262. For details of National Express coaches serving Durham, call 0191 261 6077.

Considering that Neville's Cross has developed into a suburb of Durham, the battlefield, on the western perimeter of the built-up area, remains relatively open. However, this will change if the proposed Durham western by-pass becomes a reality. It will run parallel with the Great North Road on a line north and south of the footpath to Arbour House, leading off Toll House Road (see point C of walk). In addition to breaking up the vista, it will give birth to further problems, such as factory estate development which could lead to the disappearance of all traces of the battle site.

# 5
# THE BATTLE OF OTTERBURN
## 19 August 1388

## *Introduction*

Hadrian's Wall, erected along a conveniently narrow stretch of the country between the Tyne and Solway Firth, constituted an unnatural barrier between the peoples of the North and the South. When Scotland developed as a kingdom in its own right, during the eighth and ninth centuries, it seemed sensible to use the River Tweed as a frontier. However, the existence of vast tracts of sparsely settled moorland on either side encouraged the development of a no-man's land within which border raiding became ever more rife as the centuries wore on. It has been argued that this sporadic warfare was carried on independently of national politics, with monarchs of both kingdoms having little control over their barons, yet they were not above using such rivalries to further their own ends if the occasion arose.

On the English side, border strife was to become synonymous with the illustrious Percy family. The first Percy, who came over with William the Conqueror, was granted lands in the vicinity of Whitby. Although, by the thirteenth century, the name of Percy was feared by the Scots, it was not until the death of Edward I, in 1307, that Northumberland came within the Percy grasp. By promising to secure the succession for Edward's son, Henry Percy was permitted to purchase Alnwick Castle which he developed into one of the strongest fortresses in England.

Despite the Percy prowess, the Scots usually came off best in the border raids. The north of England was ill-protected and resistance to Scottish depredations was poorly coordinated, while attempts to purchase peace proved no more successful than earlier efforts to buy off the Danes. The Scots, renowned for their ferocity, were masters of guerrilla warfare, mounting swift bloody raids, against which the English seemed powerless, thus enabling Scottish war parties to raid at will, sometimes venturing as far south as Yorkshire.

The great rivals of the Percy family on the other side of the Tweed were the Douglas clan. In comparison with the Percys, the Douglases were late starters in the baronial stakes, having risen to prominence in the early fourteenth century, during the reign of Robert the Bruce. The founder of the House, Sir William Douglas, had defended Berwick against Edward I in 1296. At length, two distinct family strands would be recognized: the Black Douglases and the Red Douglases. The Black Douglases were descended from 'The Good Sir James' Douglas, faithful adherent of Robert the Bruce, who had taken his dead master's heart for burial in the Holy Land. The Red Douglases were descended from a half-brother of James, the second Earl of Douglas, who fought at Otterburn.

It is said that the Douglas family was held in such fear by the English border settlers that its members quickly assumed the mantle of bogeymen, with which mothers would threaten recalcitrant children. Lawlessness and brutality were a way of life to the Scots, with arguments between clans being settled by force of arms, and their legendary cruelty on their excursions across the Tweed was simply an extension of their behaviour at home.

Although both the Douglases and the Percys had an interest in pursuing war for their own ends, as a means of extending their own areas of influence, their activities cannot entirely be divorced from national politics. Each family owed its allegiance to a monarchy which had been responsible for its advancement. Thus, throughout the long years of border warfare, it was not forgotten that in addition to furthering its own ambitions, each side was also representing King and Country.

# *The Road to Otterburn*

There were two varieties of Scottish kings: those who were crowned as infants and those who ascended the throne as comparatively elderly men. The first Stewart king, Robert II, fell into the latter category, succeeding David II in 1371, when he was fifty-four years of age. The son of Walter, High Steward of Scotland (a title from which 'Stewart' is derived), Robert's first priority was to secure the succession for his eldest son. Immediately afterwards came the renewal of the alliance with France – which, inevitably, entailed war with England.

Hostilities between England and Scotland legitimized the on-going border warfare, so that raid and counter-raid could be carried on without causing any embarrassment to the governments of either side. Richard II of England was happy to allow the House of Percy to represent his interests on the border, very much as the House of Douglas was encouraged to bear the brunt of the struggle for Scotland.

When, in 1385, the Scots appeared to be flagging, the French sent over a contingent of knights and materials to bolster the war effort. Coldly received, the French made poor allies, the hit-and-run tactics of the Scots having little in common with the ethics of warfare according to the code of French chivalry. When they returned home, having been treated abominably by their hosts throughout their stay and wondering, no doubt, why they were risking life and limb in the support of such an ungrateful people, the Frenchmen were given a bill for the costs of their board and keep.

Desultory hostilities continued until, in the summer of 1388, the 2nd Earl of Douglas – James – amassed a substantial force in the forest of Jedburgh. The plan of campaign was assisted by the capture of an English agent who was persuaded to share his knowledge of the whereabouts and intended movements of the enemy. According to the informant, the Scottish invasion would be countered by an English raid, either via Carlisle or Redesdale – whichever of the two paths the Scots did not take. Accordingly, the Earl of Douglas decided to divide his command and confound the English stratagem by using both routes. The larger party, under Sir William Douglas, would take the Carlisle road, while the earl would lead the smaller group of around 6,000 fighting men – including the Earls of March and Moray, Sir John Montgomery with his son, Sir Hugh, and Sir William Dalzell – via the Redesdale corridor.

The earl's raid proved an outstanding successs, his relatively compact force crossing the Tyne at Corbridge and penetrating as far south as Brancepeth, to the south-west of Durham. A few days later, following the customary orgy of pillage and destruction, Douglas retreated northwards, with a view to taking Newcastle. However, thanks to a stout defence conducted by Henry Percy – Hotspur – and his brother, Sir Ralph, the attack came to naught, although Douglas did succeed in capturing Hotspur's standard. With this prize in tow, Douglas gave up the struggle and resumed his homeward march along the Redesdale route, sacking Ponteland pele on the way. The evening of 18 August found the Scots pitching camp at a spot identified today as Greenchesters, about 1 mile to the west of Otterburn.

One would imagine that the Scots would have been anxious to make good their escape and yet, the following day, an unsuccessful attempt was made to take Otterburn Tower. It has been suggested that Douglas was looking for a confrontation with the Percys, whom he knew to be on his trail. If so, then the tower would have been an important acquisition. Although Douglas may have been willing to give Hotspur a chance to recapture his standard, the real reason for any planned resistance would have been his fear that, laden with booty, his party would soon have been overtaken in less propitious circumstances.

Hotspur seems to have been kept well informed of the manoeuvres of the invaders. In the early afternoon of 19 August, he left Newcastle at the head

Greenchesters, camp-site of the Scots in the events leading up to the Battle of Otterburn. Umfraville's over-ambitious outflanking march took him in a wide sweep to the rear of the trees on the right of the picture.

of around 8,000 men, a force which included his brother, Sir Ralph, Sir Robert and Sir Thomas de Umfraville and Sir Thomas Gray. A forced march of 32 miles would bring them to their objective: the Scottish camp.

## The Battle of Otterburn

Hotspur arrived on the scene towards evening on 19 August. A detachment under the command of the Umfravilles was ordered to work its way around to the north of the Scottish position while Hotspur, with the main body, made a frontal assault. To his surprise, he found that he was attacking a campsite of servants and attendants. Douglas, it was afterwards suspected, had planted them in the direct and only line of approach so that, in the event of an attack, his fighting men would not be caught unawares. And the ruse worked for, with the English busily slaughtering the non-combatants, the Scottish knights gained valuable time to don their armour.

Marshalling his forces, and in accordance with what was probably a preconceived contingency plan, Douglas gained the high ground to the north of his main camp. Missing the Umfravilles who had taken too wide a sweep, he managed to work his way around to Hotspur's right flank on which the Scots now launched themselves. After they had recovered from their initial surprise at being taken in the rear by an enemy they presumed occupied the ground before them, the English regrouped. Yet, tired and hungry after a day's marching without food, they found themselves being pushed back gradually towards Otterburn.

By this time, the Umfraville party was arriving in the deserted camp. The problem of making their way down to the fighting was not alleviated by the fact that it was now dark, the scene illumined only by fitful moonlight. If this contingent – which now amounted to a relief column – had advanced via the lower camp to complete its outflanking manoeuvre, the Scots would have been sorely pressed. Instead, the Umfravilles worked their way around the fighting to join the English right wing – adding sufficient weight to permit a determined charge on Douglas's silken banner. It was around this banner, emblazoned with the cross of Saint Andrew, the hearts and stars of Douglas and the motto '*Jamais aryere*', that the fighting became most ferocious.

The banner acted both as a rallying point for Douglas's men and as a marker for Hotspur who fought his way desperately to where he hoped to find Douglas, who was wearing neither breastplate nor bascinet. According to Hotspur's page, who fought by his side both at Otterburn and Shrewsbury, his master achieved the revenge he had sought by felling Douglas with his own hand. This may have been partially true, allowing for Douglas having sustained several injuries during the course of the

The Douglas Pennon. The motto '*Jamais areyre*' which the pennon bears refers to the Douglas claim to lead the Scottish army into battle. The Percy pennon had been captured by Douglas at Newcastle and it was said that, in the true spirit of chivalry, Douglas delayed his retreat into Scotland to give his foe an opportunity to regain it. (National Museum of Antiquities, Scotland)

battle, but it is more likely that he was struck down by sundry men-at-arms who failed to recognize him without his armour and in the poor light. As he lay dying, screened from his army by a bracken bush, Douglas adjured Sir John Sinclair to raise his standard once more, so that friend and foe alike would think he still lived. And so, unaware of the death of their chieftain, the Scots fought on.

The turning-point came with the capture of both Hotspur and the severely wounded Sir Ralph Percy. Lacking the pugnacious leadership of the brothers, the English resistance slackened. Towards dawn, it ceased altogether and a general flight ensued. Somewhat romantically, the Scots afterwards maintained that Hotspur, having discovered that Douglas had expired, was concerned lest there be no one of sufficiently exalted rank on the Scottish side, to whom he could surrender with honour. In response, Hotspur's captor, Sir Hugh Montgomery, urged him to surrender his sword to the bush, behind which lay Douglas's remains.

Despite having fought throughout the night, the Scots managed to engage in a vigorous pursuit of the fleeing English – the attention of the pursuers being confined to men of rank, for whom ransom would be payable. The Scots had won a famous victory.

Percy's Cross. Prior to 1777, a battle stone monument reposed 150–200 yards to the north-east of the present cross, traditionally on the spot where Douglas met his death. When the 'Redewater Turnpike' – forerunner of the A696 – was being constructed, the opportunity was taken to set up a new memorial nearer to the new road. This resulted in the surviving cross, comprising a rough stone pedestal with the base of the old battle stone into which was inserted an ancient architrave from one of Otterburn Tower's fireplaces – all in all, a curiously imbalanced structure.

# The Aftermath

The Battle of Otterburn certainly caught the popular imagination and there is no shortage of contemporary and near-contemporary material. The fact that the romantic figures of Hotspur and Douglas were involved was sufficient to endow the conflict with a significance which outweighed its consequences. A century afterwards, when men mourned the passing of the golden age of chivalry, Otterburn was viewed with a nostalgia which tended to obscure the fact that the campaign had been singularly lacking in chivalric virtues.

The zealousness of the pursuit, in the immediate aftermath of the battle, must have been tempered by fears of the possible appearance of English reinforcements. (The probability that many of the English men-at-arms did escape was due more to their negligible ransom value than to any spirit of magnanimity on the part of the Scots.) Indeed, when the battle was raging, an army of 7,000 English, commanded by the Bishop of Durham, was approaching Newcastle. Realizing that his timely intervention might be crucial, the bishop set off on a moonlit march to Otterburn.

Long before the bishop's force reached the battlefield, survivors were encountered, hurrying towards the comparative safety of Newcastle's walls. Their stories of the English defeat threw most of the relief force into panic and led to wholesale desertions within the ranks. Ultimately, the bishop decided to retreat, returning on the following day at the head of 10,000 troops, most of whom carried large horns. In an apparent effort to frighten the Scots into submission, the bishop ordered all the horns to be blown in unison. As disconcerting as the general effect may have been, the invaders showed no sign of relinquishing the safety of their well defended camp. Unlike Hotspur before him, the bishop realized that the strength of the English army lay with its archers, and that the wooded terrain which Douglas had cannily selected rendered this weapon useless. In hand-to-hand combat the Scots often proved unstoppable. The old enemy could hope to gain the upper hand only by keeping them at long range by effective use of the longbow and, much later, with concentrated musket fire. Therefore, the bishop retreated for the second – and last – time.

Only now could Douglas's men attend to their casualties and to their prisoners. Contemporary estimates put the English dead at almost 2,000 with only 100 Scottish dead. These numbers must be scaled downwards and upwards respectively, the probable final figure being much more evenly balanced. The English prisoners, over 1,000 in total, presented a logistical problem which their captors solved by freeing half of them, on the promise of payment of ransom. The other half were carried over the border, along with the body of Douglas.

The Battle of Otterburn settled nothing in terms of local rivalries but, although border raids continued much as before, there was no major confrontation for the remainder of the decade. When it came, the next Douglas–Percy trial of strength, at Homildon Hill in 1402, resulted in a decisive Percy victory. Unaccountably, the Scots, led by Archibald Douglas, took up a position on the exposed Homildon (now Humbleton) Hill where they were decimated by Percy archers. Following his capture, the badly wounded Archibald joined forces with Hotspur against Henry IV. Thus, it came about that the most unlikely of events occurred a year later when Douglas and Percy fought on the same side at the Battle of Shrewsbury – and on this occasion, both were the losers.

# The Walk

**Distance:** 4½ miles (7.24 km)

Otterburn is a small community with a main street, the A696 Newcastle road, and a minor road at the western end of the village, leading to Otterburn Camp. At the opposite end, near the B6320 Bellingham road is a substantial lay-by (point A; Pathfinder 510 889930), which makes a good starting-point for motorists.

From the lay-by, walk into the village. On the right, almost opposite the B6320, is the entrance to the Otterburn Tower Hotel (point B), which was developed from the original tower besieged by Douglas into a privately owned country house before being converted to its present use.

Continue through the village and take the road to Otterburn Camp. At the end of the built-up area, on the left, is Townhead Farm (point C; Pathfinder 510 883935). (The Umfravilles' outflanking movement would have taken them to the top of this road and through the wooded grounds of the present-day Otterburn Hall.) A bridle-way leads via the farmyard and out into the battlefield area. Walk up the bridle-way and out into the field ahead – keeping close to the wall. Hotspur's line of advance would have been parallel with one's own. Negotiate the gate into the next field and continue along, again hugging the boundary. The area defined by the present-day field boundary and the copse and white (school) buildings down by the road to the left probably represents the site of the most intense fighting, with Douglas swinging round in his own, more realistic, outflanking movement in front of Otterburn Hall.

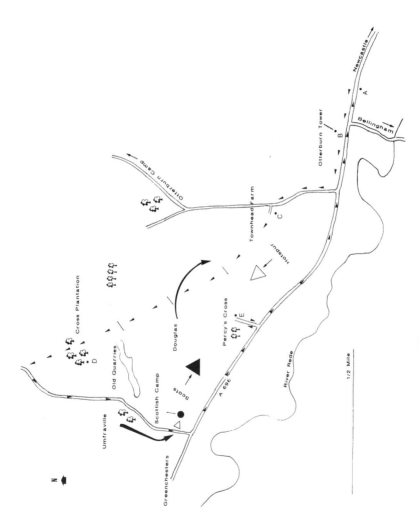

**The Battle of Otterburn
19 August 1388**

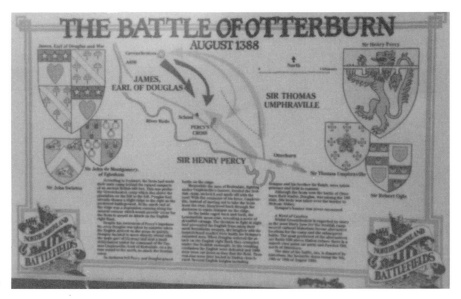

Site map of the Battle of Otterburn. The regular visitor to celebrated battlefields will be accustomed to the presence of invaluable information boards, complete with diagrams and descriptions of the action. This particular board, which can easily be missed, stands well to the rear of Percy's Cross, beyond the trees, overlooking the battlefield itself.

At the end of the second field, the course of the bridle-way becomes less apparent. Strike out for Cross Plantation (point D; Pathfinder 510 875946) ahead, exiting from the next field by means of the gate in front of the shallow, disused quarry area before Greenchesters – quite a snug site for the Scottish camp. It is necessary to bear in mind that, at the time of the battle, the whole area from Greenchesters to Otterburn Hall via Cross Plantation would have been quite heavily wooded. The bridle-way continues through Cross Plantation to join the single-track road at the other side. Walk down via Greenchesters to the main A696 road and turn to the left to return to Otterburn village.

About ½ mile down the road, past the school, is Percy's Cross (Pathfinder 510 877937), located in a copse which has been developed into a picnic area, complete with two pictorial representations of the campaign and battle (point E). Erected in 1777, the cross incorporates parts of a much earlier structure which stood in the field beyond. Continue into the village, to take well earned refreshment at the Percy Arms.

# Further Explorations

The surrounding area is rich in reminders of the importance in which it was held by the Romans. Dere Street (Pathfinder 510 878906), for instance, which borders the Northumberland National Park, linked the Roman forts of York and Newstead. Further stations were sited along the route – an example of which may be seen at nearby Blakehope (Pathfinder 510 878945). A little further south was a temporary camp, known as The Dargues (Pathfinder 510 860938). One of the finest examples of a Roman fort in Britain is at Rochester (Pathfinder 510 866986).

Abundant evidence of much earlier settlement exists in the many hillforts which pepper the Northumbrian landscape. Camp Hill (Pathfinder 510 907938) and Fawdon Hill (Pathfinder 510 896940) are two examples of hillfort sites, selected for their defensive potential. Yet human occupation of Northumbria can be traced back further still – as far as 5,000 years, to Mesolithic times, when hunters tried to eke out a living along the banks of the Tyne.

The Pathfinder 510 Ordnance Survey map depicts several settlements and field systems in the locality of Otterburn, located on rising ground, e.g. at 874964, 911908 and 901959. When, eventually, the borderers considered it comparatively safe to settle on lower ground, some form of defence was still needed and strongholds known as pele-towers or bastles developed. Surviving bastles, almost exclusively Northumbrian features, can easily be mistaken for barns – and, indeed, they were intended as places of refuge for both people and livestock. Sometimes they were built in isolation, and at other times in small groups. The valley of the River Coquet was a favourite route for Scottish raiding parties, and a group of three bastles (one of which is actually used as a barn) can still be seen in the vicinity of Raw Farm (Pathfinder 510 942980) overlooking Grasslees Burn, a tributary of the Coquet. The valley of the Rede also provided a convenient route for raiders, and the remains of a bastle are to be found to the rear of the battlefield at Otterburn (Pathfinder 510 869951).

The pele-towers were not dissimilar structures but, with the frequent addition of embattled parapets, resembled miniature castles. Also, they tended to be rather more comfortable, many being constructed as residences for Catholic priests, who might expect rough treatment at the hands of the Scots. A surviving example of priest's pele is to be found in Elsdon (Pathfinder 510 936934). A vicarage until the early 1960s, it is still in use as a residence, almost 600 years after it was built. Lewis Carroll's grandfather, the Revd Dr Dodgson, lived in the pele when he took up the post of vicar of Elsdon in 1760. He described the vestibule of his converted residence (with walls 9 ft thick) as a low stable with a kitchen above, which served as a bedroom for the curate and his wife, and the maid. Dodgson himself slept in the parlour 'between two beds to keep me from being frozen to death'.

Situated 3 miles to the east of Otterburn, Elsdon has been referred to as one of the most remarkable places in Northumberland. Another feature of the village which recalls border strife is the pair of grassy mounds known as Mote Hills (Pathfinder 510 938935). They are all that remains of a Norman castle built by the de Umfraville family (also responsible for Norham Castle) in 1080. During the nineteenth century work being carried out under the north wall of the fourteenth-century church (Pathfinder 510 937934) revealed over 100 skeletons, believed to have been the remains of some of those killed at the Battle of Otterburn.

# *Further Information*

Barrett's *Battles and Battlefields in England* contains a traditional interpretation of the battle, with Douglas's campsite being identified with a prehistoric site to the rear of Greenchesters. Burne's *More Battlefields of England* places the camp at Greenchesters. (Burne also takes issue with the near-contemporary claims that the Scottish servants' camp was situated in front of the main campsite.)

Ordnance Survey maps for the area are Landranger 80 and Pathfinder 510.

Although the battlefield is accessible via the A696 Newcastle road and the A68 Darlington–Edinburgh trunk road, motorists should allow for delays due, in part, to the proliferation of slow-moving army transport convoys operating out of Otterburn Camp.

Rail travellers should head for Newcastle (tel: 0191 232 6262). A handful of companies operate bus services between Newcastle and Otterburn. For details of these services, call 01670 533000.

There are very few battlefields which one is able to explore more fully than Otterburn. However, a recently (1994) proposed extension of the theatre of operations – in terms of rocket and artillery ranges – of the army camp to the north of Otterburn (described by the committee chairman of the Northumberland National Park as 'colossal') may impose restrictions upon the accessibility of the area.

# 6
# THE BATTLE OF TOWTON
## 29 March 1461

## *Introduction*

By 1461 Henry VI's queen, Margaret of Anjou, was recognized as the matriarch of the Lancastrian movement. Even had Henry not been captured at the Battle of Northampton in July 1460, it is likely that the autocratic and ruthless Margaret would have relegated her mild-mannered husband to a supporting role. Over the coming months and years, it seemed to matter little whether Henry were free or in captivity. Provided adequate resources were to hand, Margaret could be depended upon to prosecute her cause with vigour, although her ultimate interest lay not in restoring Henry to the throne, but in contriving to secure the succession for her son, Prince Edward.

The Lancastrian defeat at Northampton had been assured by the treachery of Lord Grey, who deserted at a crucial moment. But they remained the strongest party in England, continuing to command the support of the vast majority of the nobility. When, some months after Northampton, Richard, Duke of York hinted strongly that he wished to take the Crown for himself, both Lancastrians and Yorkists were horrified. Henry's Yorkist captors had assured him of their loyalty, being content to reinstate themselves into positions of influence and power around a pliable monarch. In the end, Richard had to be satisfied with a compromise. On 10 October 1460, by the Act of Accord, it was agreed that Henry should remain king, but that Richard and his heirs should succeed him – a proposal with which, despite the existence of his own son, Henry had readily concurred.

Margaret was furious at this plot to disinherit her offspring. She fled westward to Harlech Castle, where, under the protection of the Earl of Pembroke, she plotted revenge. With the help of the Duke of Somerset, the Earl of Devon, the Lords Ros and Clifford, and others, she amassed a substantial army at Hull. This force, augmented as it went along, proceeded to ravage the Duke of York's estates.

On 2 December Richard, commanding a small force of perhaps 5,000 men – against an estimated 18,000 Lancastrians – marched north to quell the rising. His son, Edward, Earl of March, was busy recruiting in the west. Had Edward accompanied the duke, then the Wars of the Roses might well have been brought to a premature conclusion. The Yorkist advance guard was surprised and badly mauled by a Lancastrian detachment at Worksop, the remainder of the force reaching Sandal Castle near Wakefield on 21 December.

Both sides appear to have observed a Christmas truce, for the next action occurred on 30 December, when a Yorkist foraging party was sighted by a detachment of Lancastrians – now approaching Wakefield from the scene of their own Christmas lodging at Pontefract. The Yorkists hurriedly retired within the safe walls of Sandal before the Lancastrian advance.

Margaret, who accompanied her army, could not afford to lay siege to Sandal for fear of being surprised by Yorkist reinforcements. Richard knew that he could expect a relief column but, as he was so short of supplies, he deemed it unwise to await its arrival. Therefore, against advice, he launched an assault on the Lancastrian position on Wakefield Green. Heavily outnumbered, the Yorkists were surrounded and cut to pieces. Richard and his younger son, the Earl of Rutland, together with half his command were killed.

Margaret's army was cock-a-hoop. Unfortunately, she had no funds with which to pay them and so, instead of being able to consolidate her victory, she had to stand by while her soldiers rewarded themselves for their efforts on her behalf, by embarking on an orgy of rape and pillage.

# The Road to Towton

It would have taken a day or two for news of the Battle of Wakefield and the death of his father and brother to reach the Earl of March whom, overnight, through the fortunes of war, had become head of his House and Yorkist heir to the crown. By the end of January, he was ready to set out to join Warwick. He had reached Gloucester when he learned that the Earls of Pembroke and Wiltshire had mustered an army in Wales. Turning back, Edward met them at Mortimer's Cross, near Ludlow, and won a decisive victory. Although the leaders escaped, Pembroke's father, Owen Tudor – grandfather of the future Henry VII – was captured and beheaded in Hereford. Mortimer's Cross has been dismissed as an unimportant battle, but it was one which Edward had to win in order to avoid running the risk of being caught between two Lancastrian armies.

Margaret, meanwhile, was marching down from Scotland, at the head of a Scottish army, which she had acquired in exchange for the fortress of Berwick – thereby supplying the Scots with a useful base from which to mount border raids against the strongly Lancastrian north country. Warwick had reached London – without Edward, who had been delayed through his encounter at Mortimer's Cross – and decided to halt the queen's progress at St Albans. Although the Yorkist archers inflicted severe casualties on the Lancastrians, the superior tactics of the Lancastrian commanders, Somerset and Andrew Trollope – the latter, the most underrated general of his era – won the day. King Henry, brought along by Warwick, was rescued, while Warwick himself escaped to meet Edward at Burford five days later.

As at Wakefield, Margate failed to follow up the victory. The citizens of London were terrified at the prospect of having their city sacked by the queen's wild northern army. And Margaret did not wish to risk sacrificing the citizens' goodwill by subjecting them to the ordeal, so she withdrew into Yorkshire, thereby providing Edward and Warwick with the opportunity of entering London instead – which they did on 27 February 1461. A few days later, on 4 March, he was proclaimed Edward IV, but he refused to be crowned until such time as Henry and Margaret were either dead or in exile.

The ratification of his position gave the Yorkists the advantage which Henry had but lately held – that of raising an army in the name of the king. It also made the matter of raising the necessary finance much easier. A call went out to all men between the ages of sixteen and sixty, pardons being offered to anyone anxious to consider changing sides. Merchants prepared to advance money for supplies were found, and the campaign to eliminate the Lancastrians got under way.

The Yorkist commanders' departure from the capital was staggered. Warwick left on 7 March, his brother, Lord Fauconberg, on 11 March and Edward on 13 March. Towards the end of the month, all three, having gathered more support on the way, linked up at Pontefract.

Margaret, on the other hand, suddenly found herself on the defensive. Her rabble army was still looting and pillaging – an exercise which Edward studiously avoided – yet she experienced no difficulty in attracting new recruits to her cause. Hearing of the approach of Edward, she left Henry in her headquarters – at York – and marched out to meet him, her army pitching its tents on Towton Heath. (Although he is often depicted as being in an advanced stage of senility, Henry was still only thirty-nine years old.)

A detachment of Yorkists under Lord Fitzwalter had secured the ford over the River Aire at Ferrybridge. Having learned of this, Lord Clifford resolved to take it for the Lancastrians. At dawn on 27 March, he swept down on the unsuspecting outpost, which was wiped out to a man. Edward's efforts to retake the ford by direct assault failed, so he despatched a column further upstream, to Castleford, where they could cross and take Clifford in the rear.

Edward IV. This representation of the victor of the Battle of Towton is taken from a woodcut by John Rastell and was included in his *Pastime of the People*, published in 1529. Rastell was both a printer and a lawyer, who based his work very largely upon Robert Fabian's *New Chronicles of England and France*.

Anticipating the stratagem, Clifford pulled back towards Towton, but had the misfortune to run into an advance guard of Yorkists at Dinting Dale, near Saxton. As he had surprised Fitzwalter at Ferrybridge, so was he now taken unawares and, in a sharp fight, he lost his own life. When the main body of Yorkists arrived on the scene, it was decided to make camp at Saxton.

On the morning of 29 March 1461 the two armies, drawn up in a line a mile in length, came face to face. Church bells were ringing, for it was a Sunday – Palm Sunday. And it began to snow.

# The Battle of Towton

Considering its importance in terms of establishing a dynasty (albeit short-lived), comparatively little is known about the course of the battle. However, it is reasonably certain that the 40,000-strong Lancastrian army was drawn up to the south of Towton – probably in three divisions. It is also possible that a detachment lay in ambush to the south-west, in the present-day Castle Hill Wood. According to C.R.B. Barrett in *Battles and Battlefields in England*, the Duke of Somerset commanded the Lancastrian centre, with the Earl of Northumberland on the right and the Earl of Devon on the left. In a paper prepared for the *Yorkshire Archaeological and Topographical Journal*, however, Clements Markham insists that Northumberland led the centre, with the Earl of Devon on the right and Lord Dacre on the left. Somerset is relegated to command of a reserve division based at Towton. In any event, the Lancastrian lines were tightly packed.

Facing them, to the north of Saxton, were around 36,000 Yorkists. Again, the nature of their deployment remains unclear. However, Lord Fauconberg may have commanded the centre, with Edward and the Earl of Warwick on the wings. A further Yorkist contingent under the Duke of Norfolk was lagging behind and would not reach the battlefield before noon.

It was Fauconberg who commenced hostilities by pushing forward his archers, who fired a few controlled volleys into the massed Lancastrian ranks and then withdrew. The Lancastrian archers returned fire but, in view of the fact that they did not move up, their arrows fell short. Advancing a second time, Fauconberg's men were able to retrieve them.

The damage done by the Yorkist bowmen seems to have been sufficient to spur the Lancastrian army into action. Pushing forward against driving snow, they suffered heavy casualties as a result of a steady, accurate fire maintained by the archers. At length, the Yorkist line also advanced, savage hand-to-hand fighting ensuing as both sides closed – the legendary ferocity of the encounter being due to the fact that Yorkist and Lancastrian were under instructions to give no quarter to the enemy.

This trial of strength may have continued until mid-day and the Yorkists could well have been the worse for wear, particularly if an assault directed against their left flank from the cover of Castle Hill Wood materialized. And then, just when it seemed that the Yorkist line must give way, the Duke of Norfolk finally arrived on the scene with enough weight to bolster the flagging right wing, but insufficient to turn the tide in a spectacular manner. And so, for the better part of the day, the battle-weary troops fought on. At some point in the afternoon, Lord Dacre, pausing to take a drink of water, removed his helmet and was killed by an arrow fired, some said, by a boy who recognized Dacre as the man who had killed his father.

Who knows why fortune favours one side as opposed to another in determining the outcome of a battle? Perhaps victory can depend upon one man making a conscious decision to hold his ground, and defeat upon the

Lord Dacre's Tomb. The restored tomb is situated on the north side of All Saints' churchyard, Saxton. A tradition to the effect that Lord Dacre was buried standing upright, alongside his horse, was confirmed during the nineteenth century when the grave was disturbed. The remains of many combatants of more humble birth were laid to rest with less ceremony to the rear of the tomb, along the north wall.

same man turning upon his heels. On this Palm Sunday at Towton, it was the Lancastrians who began to steal away, at first – singly and in pairs – unnoticed. Unchecked, the exodus developed into a steady trickle and, finally, into mass flight.

Most of the Lancastrian losses were sustained during this disorderly retreat and much has been written concerning the possible locations of the greatest slaughter. A beaten army pursued by an enemy intent on its destruction deteriorates into a collection of individuals, each anxious to save himself. And so it is improbable that the vanquished pondered overlong on the question of the best escape route. Some of those on the left wing, though sorely pressed, tried to reach York, 10 miles away, across country – and pursuit went on almost to the gates of the city itself.

The Lancastrian centre attempted a more orderly retreat to Tadcaster, via Towton, crossing the River Cock by a modest bridge – hopelessly inadequate for the occasion – on the present-day Old London Road. The icy waters, swollen by the winter rains, claimed many lives as the exhausted infantry, weighed down with armour, attempted to scramble across on either side.

The right wing had very little chance of escape, sheer pressure of numbers forcing it directly back on to the River Cock and the surrounding treacherous marshland. Those who tried to ford the river at Cocksford met a similar fate to their comrades at the bridge, with piles of corpses forming a human bridge for the convenience of the pursuing Yorkists.

In a little over ten hours, the Red Rose had been dealt a blow from which many thought it could never hope to recover.

# The Aftermath

The total number of dead was reckoned at between 26,000 and 28,000. Even the lower number may be rather high, but in attempting to rationalize the customary exaggerated figures, care should be taken not to underestimate the total which would have reflected the size of the armies involved. Similarly, the victors, ever keen to minimize their own losses were proposing Yorkist casualties of under 1,000. However, one must not be over-anxious to redress the balance, taking into account the considerable damage sustained by an army in panic-stricken flight. Lancastrian knights, burdened with heavy armour, were compelled to stand and fight. The pursuit itself was a particularly bloody one, and if a notional figure of 20,000 were taken, then the ratio would have been in the region of 8,000

Yorkist dead against 12,000 Lancastrians. As some European commentators noted gleefully at the time, it would be a long time before England would be able to prosecute any overseas wars due to the vast numbers killed at Towton.

To some, Edward was an avenging angel, the liberator of a people who had languished under the harsh rule of an unjust, overbearing pretender. Others ascribed the popularity of Edward and Warwick largely to the fact that they were the victors. With uncanny prescience a contemporary chronicler, Prospero di Camulio, drew attention to the necessity of apprehending the leading Lancastrians, notably Henry and Margaret, in order to reduce the risk of further disturbances. And if they were taken, he continued, it would not be long before recriminations broke out between Edward and Warwick.

Identification of the dead upon a field of battle was always a problem. The count at Towton included a dozen barons and over forty knights. The best that a common man could hope for was interment in one of the pits dug for mass burials on the battlefield itself. It was reported that those who were slain during the flight to York remained unburied for some time afterwards, their bodies remaining where they had fallen over a distance of 6 miles.

Somerset and Exeter made good their escape – the only Lancastrian commanders to do so. The Earl of Devon was taken prisoner. When Edward entered York in triumph, he removed what little remained of his father, the Duke of York's, head from Micklegate Bar, where it had been impaled since the Yorkist defeat at Wakefield three months before, and replaced it with the heads of Devon and others.

The first parliament of the new reign – Edward was crowned on 28 June – met on 4 November 1461. Its purpose was to stress the right of Edward to the Crown and to pass an Act of Attainder against no less than 113 of his opponents, from earls to knights and from squires to yeomen, who were stripped of their estates and thrown into poverty. Interestingly enough, the new king sought no money from this parliament, and none was provided.

The following year, the first of many conspiracies was uncovered. The Earl of Oxford had written to Henry and Margaret (who had taken refuge in Scotland) outlining a scheme which would culminate in Edward's murder. The dastardly act would coincide with coordinated invasions made by Pembroke and Somerset, from across the Channel, and by Henry, from north of the border. Oxford's messenger allowed Edward to see the incriminating correspondence, enabling him to have Oxford and the other ringleaders executed. A victory on the battlefield – even one as conclusive as that of Towton – brought with it no guarantee of a lasting peace.

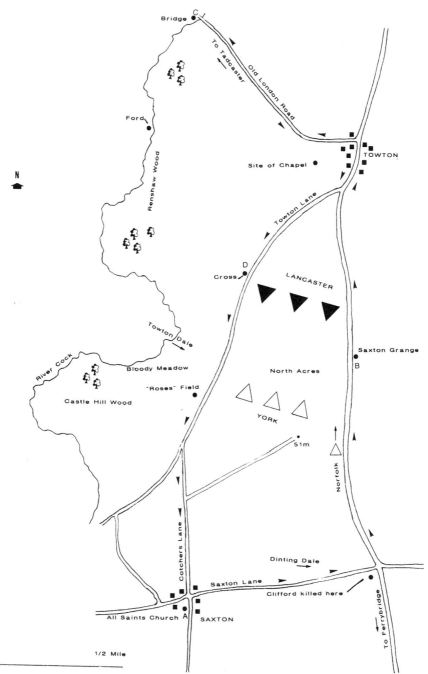

Bridge

To Tadcaster

Old London Road

Ford

Renshaw Wood

N

Site of Chapel

TOWTON

Towton Lane

Cross

D

LANCASTER

Towton Dale

Saxton Grange

B

River Cock

Bloody Meadow

North Acres

"Roses" Field

Castle Hill Wood

YORK

51m

Norfolk

Cotchers Lane

Dinting Dale

Saxton Lane

Clifford killed here

To Ferrybridge

All Saints Church  A  SAXTON

1/2 Mile

## The Battle of Towton
## 29 March 1461

# *The Walk*

**Distance:** 5½ miles (8.9 km)

This walk could be started either in Towton or Saxton. If travelling by car, the latter is preferable because the minor road widens out by the church and parking is easier than on the A162 which runs through Towton. So, begin outside the church (point A; Pathfinder 684 476369) and walk north towards the staggered crossroads, to turn right down the single-track road known as Saxton Lane. On the left-hand side, just beyond the last of the houses, is a public footpath. Unfortunately, it is not maintained. If it were, it would be possible to walk up towards what would have been the rear of the Yorkist lines. However, if this path were to be taken, there are features of interest along Saxton Lane which would be missed.

For example, the lane runs through Dinting Dale – where Clifford's command was caught and destroyed when retiring from Ferrybridge. Saxton Lane terminates in a crossroads. Ahead is a track to Scarthingwell, with the A162 Tadcaster–Ferrybridge road running north–south. Turn to the left, towards Towton. The road is a busy one, but a narrow, hard path develops in the grass verge on the right-hand side and there are lay-bys at intervals along the route.

Looking up towards the battlefield, it can be seen that Dinting Dale forms a very sharp backdrop to the rear of the Yorkist right flank. Indeed, the land tends to fall away towards the road all the way along. Norfolk's Yorkist reinforcements, arriving some hours after the start of the battle, would have had no clear picture of how things were going. Opposite Saxton Grange Farm (point B; Pathfinder 684 485382) is the field known as North Acres, where Lord Dacre met his death.

Continue on into Towton. At the north end of the village, turn left by the Rockingham Arms (Pathfinder 684 485397) along the single-track Old London Road. A little way down, on the left, is Towton Hall and behind it, Chapel Hill (Pathfinder 684 483395), site of a chapel – never completed – built by Richard III and dedicated to all who fell in the battle. It is believed that many of the dead are buried here. The track, it will be noted, veers sharply to the right. It may be that, at the time of the battle, it was possible to continue straight on to the ford situated to the south of Cocksford Hall. A pleasant walk of ½ mile brings one to the bridge (point C; Pathfinder 673 475404) around which so many fleeing Lancastrians died in their efforts to effect a crossing of what was then a raging torrent of a river. Having attained the bridge, retrace your steps, emerging once more on to the A162. Turn to

Lord Dacre's Cross. Set up in 1928, the monument is topped by a medieval cross head. For many years, this stone fragment lay in a hedge and is probably a relic from the vanished memorial chapel established by Richard III. The Lancastrian army was deployed in the fields beyond.

the right and, at the southern end of the village, take the road which branches off to the right – the B1217 to Wakefield.

The right-hand grass verge is wide and walkable. Across the fields to the right are the remains of Renshaw Wood, behind which flows the River Cock. Lord Dacre's Cross, commemorating the battle, is sited on the right-hand side of the road, at the junction with a farm track (point D). For many years, the top of the cross – which may have originated in Richard III's chapel – lay in a hedge. It was incorporated into the present monument in 1928.

One of the most intriguing topographical features of the battlefield is the undulating nature of the land. The rolling landscape, dipping unexpectedly in places, must have facilitated much localized combat. (If the fields over to the left have been ploughed recently, then it is possible that groups of treasure seekers armed with metal detectors will be in evidence. From time to time, the occasional 'find' is turned up.)

Continuing along the B1217, the easily recognizable Towton Dale now comes into view. An enclosed meadow, in which sheep are often to be seen grazing peacefully, is the Field of the White Rose and the Red. According to tradition, the Towton Rose was once to be found here in profusion. A dwarf wild rose, white in colour, its petals were tinged with red, allegedly from blood shed on the battlefield. At the turn of the century, it was believed to have disappeared, but within recent years it has made something of a recovery and may be found growing along the roadside verges. Behind this field is Bloody Meadow, the scene of great Lancastrian carnage. Immediately across the road, there was once a farm track leading over the fields to a spot from which it was possible to identify the traditional site of Lord Dacre's death.

A little further along, there is a road off to the left. This is Cotchers Lane. On the right, as the fork is approached, is Castle Hill Wood, which was far more extensive at the time of the battle. The existence of a Lancastrian ambush party is feasible, but it should be remembered that the fighting may have extended over to the wood so that any detachment emerging from it would merely have joined in the general mêlée.

Turn down Cotchers Lane. On the left is a farm track which leads to a triangulation pillar and to what would have been the rear of the Yorkist position. Certainly, the Yorkists enjoyed the advantage of higher ground. Continue into Saxton, and back to the starting-point, to complete the walk with a visit to All Saints' Church. Prominent in the north side of the churchyard is Lord Dacre's railed box tomb. The base of the tomb bears the worn inscription: 'Here lies Ralph, Lord of Dacre and Gilsland. A true soldier valiant in battle in the service of King Henry VI, who died on Palm Sunday March 29 1461, on whose soul may God have mercy.' It was rumoured that he was interred in an upright position, his horse being buried with him. Subsequent excavations appear to verify both these claims.

For those seeking refreshment, it will have been noted that The Greyhound is most conveniently situated next to All Saints'.

## Further Explorations

Situated 7 miles due east of Towton is Cawood and the slender remains of Cawood Castle (Landranger 105 5737). There has been a castle at Cawood since the tenth century. For almost 700 years, it was attached to the See of York, as a palatial residence for archbishops. Many are the monarchs said to have graced its bedchambers. Edward I and Edward II both stayed here, as did Elizabeth I and Henry VIII. Catherine Howard, Henry's fifth wife, also slept at Cawood, sharing a bed with Thomas Culpeper – an act of folly which broke Henry's heart and led her to the block.

Cawood was also the scene of the most lavish banquet ever held in England. The occasion was the appointment, in 1464, of the Earl of Warwick's brother,

George Neville, to the Archbishopric of York. In an age when common folk survived on a diet of black bread and dairy produce, the gargantuan menu for the enjoyment of the county nobility included 500 deer, 1,000 sheep, 8,000 chickens, 4,000 geese, 10,000 pastries and 100,000 gallons of assorted alcoholic beverages. In 1471, following the defeat of the Kingmaker at Barnet, George was confined in the Tower of London where, doubtless, he dined rather more modestly.

Cawood's most famous prelate was Cardinal Wolsey. Dismissed from the king's service in 1529, ostensibly for his failure to secure the annulment of Henry's marriage to Catherine of Aragon, he retired to Cawood. His stay was a short one for, on 4 November 1630, he was arrested by the Earl of Northumberland. On his way to London to face trial, he stopped at Leicester Abbey, where he died – thus saving all concerned considerable embarrassment.

During the Civil War, Cawood changed hands several times. At the outbreak of hostilities, it was secured for the Royalists, but in October 1642 it was stormed by Roundhead troops from Hull. In 1643 it changed hands at least twice more, the Roundheads taking it for the last time in 1644. In 1646 it was one of the many castles which were destroyed on Parliament's orders, its stones being used to create a new residence for future Archbishops of York, at Bishopthorpe (Landranger 105 6047). All that remains of Cawood today is the gatehouse and chapel.

Between Towton and Cawood, on the north bank of the River Wharf, is the Nun Appleton estate (Landranger 105 5540), home of leading Roundhead general Sir Thomas Fairfax, and one of several estates in the area owned by the Fairfax family. Unlike Cromwell, Sir Thomas entertained no political ambitions. After the Civil War, he retired to what he hoped would be a life of study among his books, manuscripts and coins. It was at Nun Appleton that he met with General George Monck to discuss the terms of the Restoration. Several Fairfax monuments can be seen in nearby Bolton Percy church (Landranger 105 5341), although Black Tom Tyrant, as he came to be known after having been president of the Council of the North, lies with his wife in the church at Bilborough (Landranger 105 5346).

Tadcaster lies 2 miles to the north of Towton (Landranger 105 4843). The town bridges the gap between the industrial West Riding of Yorkshire and the more sedate, agricultural North Riding. Standing on the east–west Roman road between Ribchester and York, it was certainly the Calcaria of the Roman occupation. King Harold halted here on his way to Stamford Bridge and the town was the scene of bitter fighting during the Civil War years. A mile or so to the north-west of the town is Newton Kyme (Landranger 105 4644), another seat of the Fairfax family. At Hallowe'en the ghost of Sir Thomas Fairfax has often been seen riding in the grounds of Newton Kyme Hall.

# Further Information

All the standard battlefield histories include chapters on the Battle of Towton. One of the most entertaining accounts is to be found in Richard Brooke's *Visits to Fields of Battle in England of the Fifteenth Century*, while one of the most penetrating is provided by A.H. Burne in *British Battlefields*. A.D.H. Leadman's account in *Battles Fought in Yorkshire* combines both these qualities.

Ordnance Survey maps for the area are Landranger 105 and Pathfinder 684. A small portion of the walk, between Old London Road and the River Cock runs on to Pathfinder 673, which is non-essential.

The battlefield lies mid-way between York and Leeds, tucked away between the A162 Tadcaster–Ferrybridge road and the B1217, which develops into the A642 to link Towton and Wakefield. It is easily accessible from the A1, with which it follows a parallel course to the east.

Unusually for a rural area, the battlefield is reasonably accessible by rail. There are stations at Church Fenton (2½ miles from Saxton) and at Ulleskelf (2½ miles from Towton). Both lie on the York–Leeds and York–Sheffield lines. For details of services, call 01904 642155.

Long-distance coach travellers can reach Tadcaster, 2½ miles from Towton, via the Liverpool–Newcastle Coachlink service (tel: 0151 709 6841 (Liverpool) or 0191 261 6077 (Newcastle)).

For refreshment, in addition to The Greyhound in Saxton and the Rockingham Arms in Towton, there is also the Crooked Billet, which lies to the east of Saxton on the B1217 (Pathfinder 684 464368) – an inn with a battlefield connection, as an earlier inn on this site is believed to have been the Yorkist headquarters.

# 7
# THE BATTLE OF HEXHAM
## 25 April 1464

## *Introduction*

One of the most intriguing aspects of the Wars of the Roses concerns the resilience of both York and Lancaster. After a crushing defeat on the battlefield, with casualties numbered in thousands, it would seem that one side or the other had won *the* decisive contest. And yet, sometimes within weeks, the beaten opposition would reappear in the field, having managed to raise yet another redoubtable army – and this despite the constraints imposed by a total – and declining – population of something under 2.5 million. The year 1461 alone had witnessed three major confrontations: Mortimer's Cross (2 February), St Albans (17 February) and Towton (29 March) – in all, involving around 100,000 men, of whom up to one-third may have perished. Following this exhaustive display of hostility, it is little wonder that both sides were desperately in need of a breathing space. It is not uncommon for modern historians to play down the extent of the disruption caused by the major Wars of the Roses' battles, yet 1461 must have been a particularly wretched year for many.

In addition to the famous set-piece battles, there was almost continuous fighting, albeit on a small scale such as the feud involving the Nevilles and the Percys in the north, and the bickering between the Boleyns and the Courtneys in the West Country. Such rivalries were a way of life, but none the less constituted a distressing experience for folk dependent upon these great families for their livelihoods. Following the disaster at Towton, although localized hostilities continued, it was to be three years before the Lancastrians were able to mount a serious challenge to the rule of Edward IV.

In order to do so, Queen Margaret found it necessary to seek support from France and Scotland. Both the French and the Scots were always keen to encourage internal strife in the country of the common enemy and, in giving their support to the Lancastrians – the underdogs at that moment – they had such an aim in mind. Margaret was provided with an army of a few hundred men, led by a fine soldier, Pierre de Breze. Louis had not acted out of charity, for Margaret had mortgaged Calais to him for 20,000 gold livres, and she may have had cause for complaint about the paltry force with which she had been provided. Doubtless she hoped to augment the number when she landed.

Arriving near Bamburgh on 25 October 1462, Margaret was heartened when the castle opened its gates to her. With Dunstanburgh and Alnwick following suit, Edward hurriedly amassed an army of his own, marching north at the head of 30,000 troops. Having failed to attract the degree of support she needed, Margaret decided to retreat into Scotland with her miniature invasion fleet. Setting sail on 13 November, she was beset by severe storms in the North Sea. Her own ship sank, taking with it all her belongings. Accompanied by de Breze, she reached the safety of the Berwick shore in a fishing boat. Four hundred of her French troops were driven on to the island of Lindisfarne, where they were slaughtered by the local squire.

Edward was unable to capitalize on the event because he had contracted measles, and the Yorkist command devolved upon Warwick, who laid siege to the three rebellious fortresses. By Christmas, Bamburgh and Dunstanburgh had been starved into surrender, but the appearance of a Scottish army outside Alnwick persuaded Warwick to allow the garrison to leave, unmolested.

To try to secure Northumbrian loyalty in the future, Edward forgave such Lancastrian nobles as were caught in the fortresses. The Duke of Somerset and Sir Ralph Percy, for example, had their estates restored to them, Percy being entrusted with the management of Bamburgh and Dunstanburgh. The following April, Edward realized he had made an error of judgement when, once again, Percy transferred his allegiance to the Red Rose by opening up both castles to supporters of Henry VI. In another act of treachery, Sir Ralph Grey seized Alnwick and Margaret, with James III of Scotland and 4,000 Scots augmenting the dwindling French division, laid siege to Norham Castle. When confronted by a hastily assembled Royal army, they fled – Margaret seeking refuge in Flanders, Henry with the Scots. Edward made no attempt to retake Bamburgh, Dunstanburgh and Alnwick. Instead, that autumn, he resorted to diplomacy. By Christmas, he had succeeded in depriving the Lancastrians of French and Scottish support, which left them ripe for the picking when the fighting season opened in the spring of 1464.

# The Road to Hexham

Having been betrayed by Sir Ralph Percy, one would have thought that Edward would have been rather more circumspect where the Duke of Somerset was

The Marriage of Henry VI and Margaret of Anjou. The portrait, by an unknown artist, is quite revealing, depicting Henry as a devoted husband – which was quite true. Margaret, however, was far from being the demur damsel shown here. Always the dominant partner in the relationship, it was she and not Henry who became the focal point of the Lancastrian cause. (Hulton Deutsch)

concerned. Throughout the winter of 1643, however, the king had continued to treat the duke as a loyal companion, often entrusting his personal safety to him and his men. It was not until Somerset had made an unsuccessful attempt to take Newcastle that Edward realized, at long last, the folly of his ways.

At Easter 1644 Edward had arranged for representatives to meet with the Scots at York, to conclude their agreement. He knew that, in the long run, it was a treaty which they would be unlikely to keep, but by the time they were ready to renounce it, he hoped to have mopped up any remaining pockets of Lancastrian resistance. A modest force under Lord Montagu was sent into Northumberland to meet the Scottish envoys at Norham and escort them to York. Hearing of this, and anxious to scupper the peace talks in any way possible, Somerset laid a trap for Montagu outside Newcastle. Forewarned, Montagu chose an alternative route to Newcastle, where he was amply reinforced by a 'great fellowship'.

Somerset, meanwhile, had retreated to Alnwick (where Henry VI was now in residence, having been expelled from Scotland) where he acquired his own reinforcements, which gave him command of perhaps 2,000 to 3,000 men, with which he tried to bar Montagu's road to Norham. The two armies met on 26 April, 6 miles south-east of Wooler, at Hedgeley Moor. The Lancastrians were ranged out across the Devil's Causeway, the old Roman road which sliced its way, in a perfectly straight line, through the Northumbrian countryside.

Contemporary accounts of the Battle of Hedgeley Moor, and of the events leading up to it, are sketchy, and Somerset's role in the fight is not clear. According to some authorities, the Lancastrians had two armies, Somerset being with the second one at Hexham. Leading Lancastrians who do appear to have been present included Sir Ralph Percy, and the Lords Hungerford and Ros. The latter pair are recorded as having fled the field as soon as Montagu's numerically superior force came into view, leaving Sir Ralph and a handful of personal retainers at the Yorkists' mercy.

It may be that there was little to tell, with Montagu merely closing in on those few who stood their ground. The centre-piece of the fighting seems to have comprised a valiant single-handed charge by Sir Ralph, which ended when his steed was brought down, probably by an arrow discharged from a longbow. The horse had made a gigantic bound at a point henceforth graphically described as Percy's Leap. Sir Ralph himself was mortally wounded soon afterwards, his enigmatic dying words: 'I have saved the bird in my bosom' indicating that he was proud of maintaining his loyalty to Henry VI and the House of Lancaster. Percy's Cross, engraved with the family heraldic badges, marks the spot where he died. It is doubtful whether many of his men escaped, the majority being cut down in the marshland to the east of the road.

Apparently Sir Ralph's courage was admired by his opponents, all of whom left the scene 'with full sorry hearts'. His duplicity and betrayal of Edward's trust makes this attitude all the more difficult to appreciate. There seems to have been something about the Percy family which warrants admiration. It may have been their fighting spirit, for they were at the forefront of wars both overseas and at home. At times, they appear to have borne sole responsibility for keeping the Scots at bay during the long, bitter years of border warfare. In any event, Edward, at least, must have been pleased to see the back of Sir Ralph.

# The Battle of Hexham

After the clash at Hedgeley Moor, Montagu continued on his way to Norham, where he met the Scots and fulfilled his mission of bringing them in to York where the hoped-for treaty was concluded. Montagu's movements immediately afterwards are unclear, but towards the middle of May, he was to be found in Newcastle. Somerset had been busy trying to cobble together an army capable of fighting a battle to retrieve the steadily deteriorating Lancastrian position, the two main difficulties in this respect being lack of funds and poor campaign management. By 1464 both Henry and Margaret were destitute and relied for their survival upon the charity of others. Promises of future reward might be dangled before prospective participants in a successful rebellion – but success was dependent upon a strong leadership, capable of giving substance and motivation to any challenge and, in this respect, the Lancastrian effort was sadly lacking. The years 1462–4 amounted to a sad tale of uncoordinated and half-hearted endeavours, doomed to end in failure.

The whereabouts of Henry and Margaret are also unknown. Henry may have been with Somerset's army which, on 14 May, was either encamped at, or approaching, Hexham Levels, 3 miles to the south-east of Hexham. On the same day, Montagu, who must have been aware of Somerset's movements, marched out of Newcastle to confront him.

Shortly after dawn on 15 May, Yorkists and Lancastrians met. Somerset's position – in a low-lying meadow close to Linnels Bridge – seems to have been chosen as much for its attractions as a camp-site, as by its suitability as a potential battlefield. It may have been that Somerset had no intention of fighting here. Even if he did plan to do so, he would have been neither the first commander nor the last to choose a position with his back to a river – in this case, the Devil's Water. Although, in the event of defeat, escape would prove difficult, there was also a positive aspect in that the Lancastrians could not be outflanked.

While it is true that several significant British battles in all periods of history have been poorly documented, there is none quite so bereft of contemporary comment and analysis as Hexham. The numbers involved were small – Montagu may have led 4,000 or so men, while Somerset would have been hard pressed to muster half that total. And, at the time, it would not have been envisaged that the outcome would result in seven years of comparative peace.

That Montagu launched an assault on Somerset's position from the high ground to the east of the campsite is quite clear, but the extent of the Lancastrian resistance remains a matter for conjecture. They had failed to make the grade at every attempt over the previous two years, so, once more, their resolve may have faltered at the final reckoning. One well orchestrated charge by Montagu, perhaps preceded by a few penetrating volleys from his archers, could have proved sufficient to scatter them.

Unlike Sir Ralph Percy at Hedgeley Moor, Somerset lost no time in making himself scarce. Henry, according to the chroniclers who argue for his presence at the battle, left well before the fight began – hardly an action to inspire confidence in men who were expected to fight and die for his cause. Hemmed in as they were, those Lancastrians who failed to reach Linnels Bridge must have paid a heavy penalty.

Somerset, who seems to have been wounded, sought refuge in the nearby Duke's House, where he was captured later in the day. Hastily conveyed to Hexham, he was executed in the market square.

# The Aftermath

The confrontation at Hexham was important because it put an end to Lancastrian resistance for seven years. But for the quarrel which broke out between Edward and Warwick, and which the Lancastrians planned to exploit, the peace would have lasted far longer.

With the death of Somerset, the White Rose was deprived of the last of its principal leaders in the north. The lesser lights, the Lords Hungerford and Ros, together with Sir Thomas Wentworth, Sir Thomas Hussey and others, were also extinguished.

The castles still in Lancastrian hands were now easily brought to heel, Dunstanburgh and Alnwick surrendering a week after the battle. Sir William Tailboys, who had captured Alnwick for the Lancastrians in the winter of 1461–2, was found hiding in a coal-mine near Newcastle, having in his possession 3,000 marks. It was rumoured that this sum had been

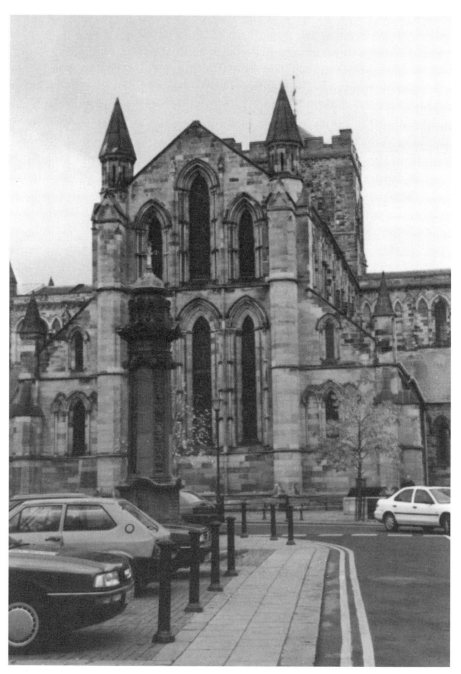

Hexham Abbey Church and Market Place. The defeated Duke of Somerset was beheaded in the Market Place and his remains buried somewhere within the precincts of the church.

intended for payment of Somerset's army but that Tailboys had resolved to use it for his own benefit. Bamburgh, with Sir Ralph Grey in command, tried to hold out, but eventually was pounded into submission by Montagu's heavy guns. Grey himself was wounded. Before his execution in Newcastle, he was degraded by having his spurs hacked off, his sword broken and his shield reversed. Edward's policy of appeasement was at an end and the executions of dozens of Lancastrian sympathizers followed.

However, both Henry VI and Margaret were still at large. Neither was in a position to pose any immediate threat, but as long as they remained at large they would constitute rallying points for future rebellions. No one knew what had happened to Henry. Rumours of his capture had been circulating from time to time since the heavy Lancastrian defeat at Towton, three years earlier. At some stage, either immediately after or a few days before the Battle of Hexham, he had fled westward – possibly in the company of some of his supporters from the north-west. (According to other, erroneous reports, he sought refuge in the east, crossing the Tyne at Bywell Castle, 6 miles from Hexham Levels.) Given shelter at Waddington Hall, near Clitheroe, he was betrayed and captured by Thomas Talbot in 1465. Tied to his horse, Henry was taken to London. Wearing a cap of straw, he was led three times around the pillory and thence escorted to the Tower, where he was to languish for the next five years.

Margaret presented a different problem. She was always ready to abandon Henry in pursuit of her own safety, but the fact that they had become separated did make Edward's task harder. Legend has it that Margaret was present at Hexham and afterwards was taken prisoner. While her captors argued over the division of her treasure, a sympathetic Yorkist took pity on her and her son, the young Prince Edward, and led them to the safety of West Dipton Wood, where they took shelter in a cave, known as Queen's Cave. But the locality was the known haunt of bandits, one of whom stumbled upon their hiding place. Admitting the identity of both herself and her son, she threw herself upon the rogue's mercy, and he helped them to safety. If this incident occurred at all, it must relate to an earlier date and an alternative location.

In fact, by the date of the battle, Margaret had already been on the continent for several months. She was in a state of abject poverty, having no money of her own. De Breze, who accompanied her, had spent his own fortune in supporting her cause, and for the next few years, she presided over an impoverished court in her father's castle in Barrois.

With Henry in the Tower and Margaret in exile, Edward was, at long last, master of his realm. He had overcome his enemies, but it remained to be seen whether he would be quite so successful in retaining his friends.

# *The Walk*

**Distance:** 5 miles (8.05 km)

The B6306 Hexham–Blanchland road is narrow and twisting, with only intermittent provision of places where it is possible to park a car. However, there is a little off-road parking between Hexham and Linnels Bridge – on the right-hand side, travelling in the direction of Blanchland. This makes a reasonable starting point for the walk (point A; Pathfinder 547 951623).

Walk up to Linnels Bridge (point B) where the road narrows to a single track – so a little care is needed. Although allegedly dating from 1531, the bridge may have been rebuilt in the late seventeenth century. Continue along the road to Linnels Farm (point C; Pathfinder 547 956615). With the permission of the farmer, follow the farm-track down to Hexham Levels, the site of the battle. It is probable that Somerset would have given his relatively small army as much width as possible by occupying the foreground, away from the river, but this did not stop his troops from wilting as the impetus of Montagu's downhill charge sent a shock-wave through the front ranks.

Return to the main road and turn to the right to continue to the junction with the B6307. To the left, the ground rises up to Swallowship Hill (Pathfinder 547 961622), a suggested alternative location for the battle. While Swallowship Hill is an excellent vantage point, commanding the Linnels Bridge crossing of the Devil's Water as well as fording points to the north-east, it would have made a poor camp-site and, had Montagu been compelled to mount an assault on this position, then the battle must surely have been far more of 'a close thing' than one is given to understand.

Continue down the B6306. To the left is a track (Pathfinder 547 960610) bordering Dipton Wood and which, if followed, would lead one to Corbridge. It is from this direction that Montagu may have advanced with his troops, which were then deployed to mount their assault on the Lancastrian position beyond the wooded area to the right, on Hexham Levels.

Continue to the public footpath, leading to Peth Wood and Whitley Chapel, on the right-hand side of the road (point D; Pathfinder 547 959603). Walk down this track which takes one through a farmyard and beyond, via the stile on the right, to skirt the wooded ravine through which the Devil's Water tumbles noisily. With such a raging torrent at their backs, it is difficult to imagine how many of the fleeing Lancastrians could have escaped, unless the intractable terrain itself discouraged pursuit.

Walk down through the woods to Linnelswood Bridge (Pathfinder 560 951598), which crosses the river at one of its less turbulent points, and walk

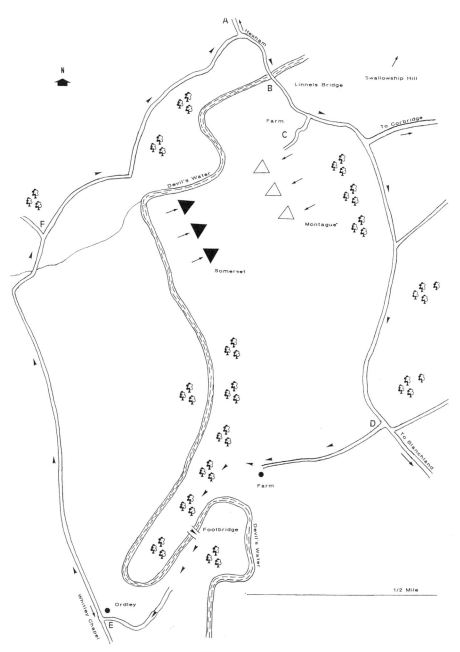

**The Battle of Hexham
25 April 1464**

up through the woods at the other side. During the summer months, the path can become quite overgrown. Upon emerging from the wood, turn to the right, onto a track which leads up to Ordley (point E; Pathfinder 560 947695) and the Hexham–Whitley Chapel road. Turn right, towards Hexham.

Continue along this road, through Newbiggin, and take the single-track road to Lamb Shield leading off to the right (point F; Pathfinder 547 945610). One is now at the rear of the battlefield, which is beyond the trees and the river to the right. Across this ground, those Lancastrians who managed to effect a crossing of the Devil's Water must have fled. Stretching away westward are the strips of woodland which develop eventually into West Dipton Wood.

Continue along the track, to emerge onto the B6306, to the north of Linnels Bridge. By turning to the left, a short walk will bring one back to one's starting-point. Refreshment may be taken at one of Hexham's excellent hostelries.

# Further Explorations

Perhaps a fitting place to begin any further exploration of the area is at Hadrian's Wall, for without it settlement of the border country would have been greatly hampered. Started at the instigation of the Roman Emperor, Hadrian, in AD 122, it took several years to complete. Running for 73 miles along the narrow neck of land between the Tyne and the Solway Firth, it consisted of a stone wall 8 ft thick and 20 ft high. The builders made use of steep escarpments which enhanced the height, or else dug deep ditches to compensate. Forts were constructed at points 17 miles apart, with smaller milecastles about 1 mile apart in between. Some 5,000 troops were needed to patrol it.

Four miles to the north of Hexham is Chesters Fort (Landranger 87 9170), which is a remarkably well preserved example of one of the forts and includes the remains of a bath house by the river. Nearby is Brunton Turret (Pathfinder 547 922699) which provides a fine view of a 70 yard stretch of the wall.

Another Roman site of importance may be seen at Corbridge where the settlement known as Corstopitum (Pathfinder 547 983648) constituted an important supply centre and base for the legions' Scottish campaigns.

Of further military interest in Corbridge itself is Vicar's Pele, a fortified tower on the south side of Corbridge Church (Pathfinder 547 988645). One of many such structures which sprang up in the border country during the fourteenth century, Vicar's Pele was built around 1300 as an ecclesiastic's residence. It consists of three storeys and an embattled parapet and, with very little allowance made for the passage of light and air, it must have presented a daunting picture to marauding Scots.

As might be expected, there are the remains of several castles in the vicinity of Hexham. The hamlet of Halton has both a Roman fort (Pathfinder 547 997683) and a medieval castle (Pathfinder 547 998678). The latter is fourteenth century in origin and, although substantially rebuilt in the early eighteenth century, the familiar square tower with four round corner turrets has survived. Nearby Aydon Castle (Landranger 87 0066) remains largely intact – and has a claim to be one of the finest fortified manor-houses in the country.

All that is left of Dilston Castle (Pathfinder 547 977633) is the ruined fifteenth-century tower. Considerable changes were wrought by the last private owner, the third Earl of Derwentwater, in the early eighteenth century. A committed Jacobite, he took part in the ill-fated rebellion in 1715. Following his execution in February 1716, his headless body was laid to rest in the chapel in the castle grounds. The ghost of Lady Derwentwater haunts the ruins.

Hexham itself is famous for its abbey (Pathfinder 547 935642), founded by Wilfrid of Ripon in AD 674. The abbey church (containing Somerset's remains) is a fine example of Early English architecture. Remains of the original structure have survived to be incorporated in the present building, despite the damage suffered at the hands of both Danes and Scots. One surviving feature is St Wilfrid's Chair, which played an important role in the rigorously enforced rights of sanctuary. Anyone who harmed a fugitive who was sitting in the chair could find himself facing the death penalty.

It is said that Hexham was the scene of the very first blood to be spilt at the beginning of the Civil War. Certainly, the town saw very little action afterwards, the most noteworthy subsequent incident being a skirmish fought in the locality in May 1644.

# Further Information

Accounts of the Battle of Hexham are rather thin on the ground. Barrett in *Battles and Battlefields of England* covers the battle in tandem with Hedgeley Moor, as does Philip Warner in *British Battlefields: The North*. The case for Swallowship Hill being the site of the battle is put by Dorothy Charlesworth in an article in *Archaeologia Aeliana*, 4th Series, Vol. 30, 1952.

Ordnance Survey maps for the area are Landranger 87 and Pathfinders

547 (covering Hexham and both suggested battlefield sites) and 560, covering the southern portion of the suggested walk.

Hexham, lying off the A69 Newcastle–Carlisle road – 41 miles from Carlisle and 17 miles from Newcastle – is very accessible. The B6306 Blanchland road is to the south of the town.

For details of British Rail services to Newcastle, call 0191 232 6262. For details of services to Carlisle, call 01228 44711. Hexham is served by the Tyne Valley Line, the coast-to-coast railway linking Carlisle and Newcastle. Call either of the above two numbers for details.

Although there is no National Express coach link, buses do operate between Hexham and Newcastle and from Hexham to Carlisle. For details, call 0191 232 4211 and 01946 63222 respectively. The starting-point for the suggested walk is a distance of about 1½ miles from the railway station.

The Tourist Information Office is situated in the Old Gaol, near the Market Place (call 01434 605225 for details of opening times), as is the Border History Museum (call 01434 652349 for details of opening times).

# 8
# THE BATTLE OF FLODDEN
## 9 September 1513

## *Introduction*

Henry VII died in 1509. The Wars of the Roses had ended with his victory at Bosworth in 1485 but, throughout his reign, he had to contend with various Yorkist challenges to his authority. In 1487 Lambert Simnel, impersonating the Earl of Warwick, had been proclaimed 'King Edward VI' by the Irish – only to see his claims dashed at Stoke Field. And as late as 1499 another imposter, Perkin Warbeck, pretending to be Edward IV's son, Richard of York, was executed following another unsuccessful attempted coup. In fact, Henry had shown remarkable persistence and cunning in hunting down and eliminating all potential Yorkist rivals. Sir James Tyrell, for example, before being executed on a trumped-up charge, had been made to confess to the murders of the 'Princes in the Tower'. The legitimate Yorkist heir, Edmund, Earl of Suffolk, survived for a time by taking refuge in Flanders, before being returned to England and imprisoned in the Tower. If surviving Yorkists hoped that the accession of a new monarch would bring an end to the persecution, then they were to be disillusioned as Henry VIII was set fair to continue the slaughter for the next thirty years.

The old enemy, Scotland, had been pacified momentarily by Henry VII. The Anglo-Scottish Treaty of 1502 provided for the marriage of his daughter, Margaret, to the Scottish king, James IV. In addition, each country agreed to aid the other in the event of war. Historians have lauded Henry's statesmanship in negotiating an agreement, but although the marriage proved a great success, the rest of the treaty was doomed to failure. Scottish border raids continued and traditional Scottish ties with England's habitual European enemy, France, were too strong to be extinguished by a signature on a piece of paper.

In 1492 a treaty had also been thrashed out with France. Entering into an alliance with Spain and the Papal States against France, Henry raised money with a view to recovering the conquests of Henry V. But instead of waging war, he concluded a separate peace with France, by which the French king, Charles VIII, agreed to pay him a substantial annual tribute. Again, this has been hailed as a brilliant diplomatic manoeuvre. In fact, Henry had let down his allies and cheated his own subjects out of the money voted for the campaign that never was.

Both these treaties were renewed by Henry VIII. The Scottish treaty was already nearing the end of what was always destined to be a short life span. English resistance to continued border depredations, coupled with retaliation against acts of piracy directed at English ships, gave James an excuse to seek to dissolve the partnership. The French treaty was also doomed when hostilities broke out between France and the combined might of Spain, the Papal States and Venice.

Cunningly cultivated by his father-in-law, Ferdinand of Spain, Henry agreed to join the Holy League against France, and a special parliament summoned in February 1512 agreed to raise funds to meet the cost of England's participation in the crusade. The campaign got off to a bad start. A poorly supplied expeditionary force under the Marquis of Dorset disintegrated through disease and lack of discipline. This was followed by a naval disaster when an English fleet – again inadequately provisioned – was easily bested by the French galleys off Brest.

Undaunted, Henry decided to take personal command of future operations, and on 30 June 1513 he arrived at Calais. As he expected, Louis had contingency plans for dealing with his personal intervention, plans which involved renewing the 'Auld Alliance' with Scotland.

# The Road to Flodden Field

If the Scots were to mount an invasion of England, then (so Louis reasoned) Henry would have to return home in order to secure the safety of the realm. Happy to oblige, James nevertheless needed continuous encouragement, in the form of men, munitions and money, and a continuous flow of each commodity acted as a signal to the English that the game was afoot. Whereas a more cautious monarch would have entertained second thoughts about embarking upon overseas adventures when danger threatened at home, the brash young Henry had sufficient confidence in his servants to leave matters in their hands.

The responsibility for organizing defences for a Scottish invasion rested with the Lieutenant-General of the North, Thomas Howard, Earl of Surrey. Henry's trust in the earl raised some eyebrows, not least because at seventy years of age he was, by the standards of the time, a very old man. Most surprising of all, considering the Tudor paranoia as far as the White Rose was concerned, Surrey was the son of John Howard, the Duke of Norfolk, who had fought and died for Richard III at Bosworth.

The septuagenarian Yorkist wasted no time in making preparations for the expected confrontation and by 21 July, he was ready to march north – and not before time, for on 26 July James sent an ultimatum to Henry, threatening to invade England if he did not lift the siege of Therouanne. Henry replied by daring James to do his worst. James's response was to mobilize the largest Scottish army ever seen. According to rumours, doubtless encouraged by the Scots themselves, it comprised 100,000 men. In reality, it cannot have amounted to more than half this number, but it was still large enough to throw the northern counties into panic. Well armed, with an experienced French contingent and a formidable artillery train, James must have considered his force as virtually unsinkable.

Surrey set out from London with little more than 500 men. Henry's army had been drawn from the southern counties, which left the earl heavily dependant upon successful recruitment en route to the border county. Arriving at Pontefract Castle at the beginning of August, he spent three weeks consolidating his position, nominating Newcastle as the mustering point for all who were instructed to rally to the defence of the realm. Travelling via York and Durham, Surrey himself reached Newcastle on 30 August. Over the next few days, a steady trickle of men from Yorkshire, Lancashire and Cheshire swelled the numbers of the army to some 20,000. In particular, Sir Edward Stanley gathered 6,500 men, while Surrey's elder son, Thomas Howard, the Lord High Admiral, with 1,000 professional soldiers, eventually caught up with the main body in the vicinity of Alnwick, to which Surrey moved on 3 September.

The Scots had actually crossed the border at Coldstream on 22 August, and rapidly reduced Norham Castle, together with the smaller fortresses of Wark, Etal and Ford. With these minor successes under his belt, James decided to await developments. These occurred with the gentlemanly exchange of heralds, whereby both sides agreed to a pitched battle by Friday 9 September at the latest. When Surrey accordingly arrived at Wooler, thinking that the Scots were still in the vicinity of Ford, he found, to his horror, that they had crossed the River Till and now occupied a seemingly impregnable position on Flodden Hill.

Indignant at what he regarded as a breach of professional etiquette, Surrey demanded that the Scots descend to level ground so as to ensure a fair contest. Their refusal to budge placed Surrey in a difficult position. His men were running short of supplies and he had to think of some ruse to force James's hand. He decided, accordingly, to outflank the Scots by moving north, a risky manoeuvre which involved organizing his army into a marching column which would be easy meat for the enemy, should they decided to launch an attack. To compound what should have been a grave tactical error, Surrey proceeded to split his force: a vanguard under son, Thomas, and a rearguard commanded by Surrey himself. Taking a wide sweep north via Duddo, Thomas recrossed the Till at Twizel Bridge in mid-morning of 9 September, while his father forded the river further south, possibly at Milford. By using two bridges, they were able to effect a crossing much more quickly – hence the reason for dividing the army.

James appeared to be not over concerned at being outflanked. Seeing no reason to desert a position of strength, he merely turned his men around and advanced from Flodden Hill to Branxton Hill, a position not much less formidable and from where the laborious English approach could be observed. At last, it appeared, the English were going to attack.

# The Battle of Flodden

As it approached the new Scottish position, the English army found its way forward blocked by Pallin's Burn and the marshland surrounding this tributary of the Till. Thomas struggled across on a causeway running through the centre, with Surrey effecting a crossing farther east. The Scots, who may have been of the opinion that Surrey's apparently absurd manoeuvres amounted to a clumsy ploy to draw them down, continued to cling to their hill-top advantage. Fearful that they would be upon him at any moment, Thomas, who was first upon the scene, sent a message to his father, begging him to make haste.

At length, the two armies faced one another, each adopting what was an unusual formation. As opposed to the customary three 'battles', both armies were divided into four divisions and a reserve unit. On the Scottish left were the Earls of Huntley and Home who faced Edmund Howard, Thomas's younger brother. The second Scottish division under the Earls of Crawford and Montrose opposed Thomas Howard. Fittingly, perhaps, King James faced Surrey, and the Earls of Lennox and Argyle opposed Sir Edward Stanley. The Earl of Bothwell and Lord Dacre commanded the Scottish and English reserves respectively.

In the late afternoon, an exchange of artillery fire began. In the event, little damage was inflicted, but after having taken such immense pains to get them to the field of battle, both sides must have been determined to make some use of their heavy guns. When a stray cannon ball killed their chief gunner, the Scots decided to take the initiative, the Earls of Huntley and Home advancing on the English right. The younger Howard brother's men

'Flodden Field'. The view from the battlefield monument on Piper's Hill, the position occupied by Edmund Howard.

crumbled under the ferocity of the Scottish assault, and it fell to Lord Dacre to stabilize the English defence with a well timed intervention.

With all the impetus provided by a downhill run, the two Scottish centre columns, supported by Bothwell's reserve, hurled themselves against their English counterparts, whose front line held firm. It had to because there was nowhere to go. Behind it lay the treacherous bog, and beyond the bog, hostile territory. Moreover, the English centre was augmented by the survivors of Edmund Howard's column, Home and Huntley having retired from the fray in the belief that they had done their duty.

The action which turned the tide of battle in Surrey's favour took place on the Scottish right. Argyll and Lennox were the last to engage the enemy, their inactivity (it has been argued) being due to Stanley's comparatively late arrival on the scene. Had the Scots, in the true chivalric manner, waited for him to take up position? If so, then their consideration was misplaced in view of the cunning employed by Sir Edward to gain the upper hand. While a portion of his column remained in situ to repel the subsequent Scottish onslaught, the remainder, with Stanley at its head, managed to approach the right flank unobserved – to devastating effect. Subjected to attack from both front and rear, the Scottish right disintegrated and fled.

The Standard of the Earl Marischal of Scotland. The standard, with the motto 'Truth Prevails', was carried into battle at Flodden. It is said to carry traces of blood of the man who carried it – John Skirland of Plewlandhill. Despite capture and imprisonment, Skirland managed to conceal it and eventually contrived to take it home to safety. (Faculty of Advocates, Edinburgh)

Stanley now turned his attention to the centre, and King James. The English billhooks had proved more than a match for the long pikes – of little value in close combat – wielded by the Scots and Stanley's charge into the rear of the king's column, in conjunction with an attack by Lord Dacre on the centre left, ended the Scottish resistance. His position now hopeless, and abandoned by the survivors of his grand army, James still fought on, surrounded by a group of fanatical supporters. One by one they were cut down until the king himself finally fell. The whole battle had been fought to a conclusion in a little over two hours.

# The Aftermath

It is often claimed that, as the last great medieval battle fought on English soil, Flodden marks a watershed in military history. Up to a point this is true, but such an argument does tend to obscure the element of continuity in the development of warfare between 1513 and 1642, when the first major battle of the English Civil War was fought at Edgehill. There were, for example, the famous Anglo-Scottish battles of the 1540s: Solway Moss, Ancrum Moor and Pinkie Cleugh. Throughout the 1590s, several significant Anglo-Irish battles took place – in which the English invariably came off worst. From time to time, war would break out with France and, if no home-grown war were available, English mercenaries would often be found fighting in European conflicts, the participants gaining much valuable experience. Many famous Civil War commanders, Prince Rupert, Sir Jacob Astley, Philip Skippon and George Monck among them, learned much from their involvement in the Thirty Years' War, for example.

Whatever might be said about Flodden in the long-term, its immediate results were clear-cut. The Scottish dead numbered 10,000, and it has been said that a list of those slain would amount to a catalogue of the ancient nobility. The lives of a dozen earls, the Archbishop of St Andrews and many heads of families of distinction were brought to an abrupt end. Despite pleas for mercy and offers of ransom, few prisoners of any standing were taken. Mindful of the legendary displays of cruelty which invariably accompanied the Scottish border raids, the English mood was not one of benevolence. Even as they retreated, the invaders engaged in as much plundering as their weakened condition allowed. They robbed their own dead and dying comrades and even turned on their French allies whom, in their fury, they blamed for their defeat. The morning after the battle, Thomas Howard was securing seventeen abandoned enemy guns when a small body of Scots appeared on a hill. Howard put them to flight by turning their own artillery on them.

In addition to these guns and a variety of small arms and equipment, the victors removed what was believed to be James's corpse from the field. Afterwards, maintaining that it was the wrong body, the Scots circulated a story to the effect that their king had escaped and was travelling in the Holy Land, from whence he would return at a propitious moment. However, despite being fearfully mutilated, the corpse in question was identified by those who had known James well. Subsequently embalmed, it was, some claim, finally laid to rest in the monastery at Sheen. Others are of the opinion that, having occupied a lumber room for many years, it was thrown into a common grave.

On the English side, perhaps as few as 2,000 casualties were sustained. The Earl of Surrey became Duke of Norfolk and Sir Edward Stanley was made Lord Monteagle while, in Scotland, a one-year-old infant succeeded to the throne as James V, the future father of Mary, Queen of Scots.

The invasion had been a total failure. A large, well equipped army had been destroyed by one half its size and, along with it, the king and the flower of Scottish nobility. Instead of relieving pressure on France it had, if anything, strengthened Henry's hand. News of the victory reached him on 25 September. A few weeks earlier, with the aid of Austrian mercenaries, Henry's army had routed the French at Guinegate, a fight which came to be known as the Battle of the Spurs because of the speed of the French retreat.

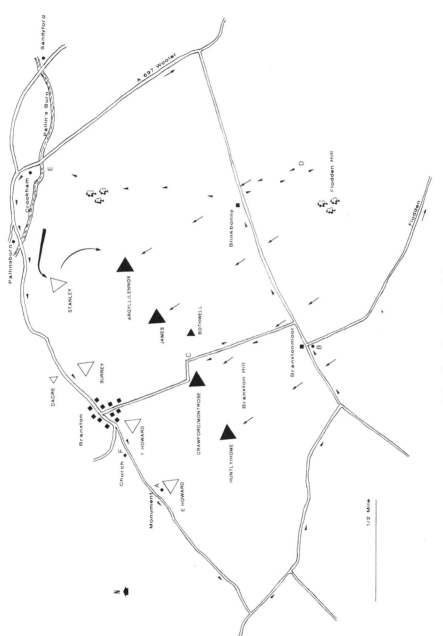

Pallinsburn

Sandyford

Pallin's Burn

A 697 Wooler

Crookham

E

Flodden Hill

D

Blinkbonny

Flodden

STANLEY

ARGYLL/LENNOX

JAMES

BOTHWELL

SURREY

DACRE

Branxton

C

CRAWFORD/MONTROSE

Branxton Hill

Branxtonmoor

B

T HOWARD

Church F

HUNTLY/HOME

Monument A

E HOWARD

N

1/2 Mile

**The Battle of Flodden
9 September 1513**

These famous back-to-back victories were the occasion for great celebrations in which Henry, we are told, spent whole nights dancing with the ladies of the Austrian court – a time of gaiety and laughter to which his thoughts must often have returned in the troubled years to come.

# The Walk

**Distance:** 9 miles (14.48 km)

Begin at the Battlefield Monument (point A) to the west of the village of Branxton, where ample off-road parking is available (Pathfinder 463 889373). The monument stands on the ridge of high ground – Piper's Hill – on the extreme right of the English position on a spot occupied by Edmund Howard. People visiting the battlefield for the first time often arrive with the expectation of finding a much higher, rough moorland site. In fact, the ground today is well cultivated and the site occupied by the English is only around 250 ft above sea-level, fronted by a comparatively gentle gradient which the Scottish infantry was able to negotiate without much difficulty, to sweep aside Howard's men.

Leaving the monument site, turn to the left, walking away from Branxton. Upon reaching the T-junction, turn to the left to begin the ascent of the sharply rising ground towards Branxton Hill. The crest of the hill over the fields to the left of the road is 500 ft in height and, as may be observed, represents a position of some strength.

At the next T-junction, turn to the left again. Some 500 yards along this road, another single-track road branches off to the right (point B) towards Flodden. One can see how steeply the land rises to Flodden Edge – again, a remarkably strong position for the Scots, who descended the hill to cross the plain, now dissected by the road, to reach Branxton Hill.

Walk past the junction and a little further along on the left is a road leading back to Branxton. Turn down this road which crosses the ground between the two hills in order to follow in the footsteps of the Scottish army. Walk along as far as the bend (point C; Pathfinder 463 898369) in order to look down on Branxton Village and the monument. From the heights of Branxton Hill, the English situation must have appeared desperate. As the English left gave way under the impetus of the charge of Home's borderers, it must have seemed to James that the day belonged to him – and so he abandoned his position.

After retracing one's steps, one may continue along the road towards the A697, until one reaches a bridle-way on the right, opposite Blinkbonny. .This track leads up to Flodden Hill (point D) and the original Scottish position – a steep climb, but well worth it. Return to the road once more.

The Battlefield Monument, Branxton.
The monument on Piper's Hill in the
failing light of an autumn afternoon.

Almost opposite is another well defined track running over the fields to link
up with the A697 at Crookham (point E). Both Stanley and Surrey would
have crossed Pallin's Burn nearby. The track joins the A697 just before the
bridge over Pallin's Burn. Walk along the A697 and, at the Branxton turn-
off, pause for refreshment at the Bluebell Inn before continuing into the
village and beyond, to the monument.

Pause at the modest Church of St Paul (point F). Remodelled in 1849,
little remains to remind one of its Norman origins. It was here that King
James's body was brought the day after the battle, before being taken to
Berwick-upon-Tweed and thence to London.

Continue along the road to the monument and the starting-point.

## Further Explorations

The castles which the Scots took soon after crossing the border – at Norham,
Wark, Etal and Ford – were just four of several Anglo-Scottish border
fortresses which were essential to the security of an area which languished in

perpetual fear of rapine and pillage at the hands of raiding parties. Having suffered for centuries from the depredations wreaked by Viking incursions, perhaps the Northumbrians had come to accept the risks as part and parcel of their way of life.

Norham Castle (Landranger 74 9047), originally a wooden structure erected by Bishop Flambard in 1121, belonged to the Bishops of Durham who kept their treasury here and presided over the tract of land then known as Norhamshire. Set on a promontory in a curve of the River Tweed, it was one of the strongest border castles. Under attack on many occasions (notably in events leading up to both the Battle of the Standard and the Battle of Flodden, when it was badly battered by King James's heavy guns) it suffered much damage and was under continual repair. It is said that the castle fell to James through the treachery of a defender who pointed out its weakest point – the Scottish king rewarding his benefactor by having him hanged.

One of the legends of Norham may also have inspired Sir Walter Scott's *Marmion*. At some time during the fourteenth century, Sir William Marmion of Scrivelsby in Lincolnshire received a gift of a golden helmet from a lady who bade him wear it in the most dangerous place in England. Such was his regard for the lady in question – and such was the reputation of the border country – that Sir William set out immediately for Norham Castle. Shortly after his arrival, he was encouraged to face, single-handed, a band of Scots from Berwick, intent on mischief. Wearing his golden helmet, he sallied forth and although he gave a good account of himself, he was eventually unhorsed. Fortunately, all ended well for the Norham garrison arrived on the scene in the nick of time, and the Scots were sent packing.

During the Civil War, notwithstanding its strategic position, Norham was garrisoned by neither Royalists nor Roundheads, although it is believed that Cromwell did lodge here in September 1648.

Of Wark Castle (Landranger 74 8238) there is nothing to be seen, apart from a grassy mound, although this also was one of the most important of the border strongholds. From 1150 to 1295, when the area was under Scottish rule, the Kings of Scotland held court here. Later, when Tynedale was part of England, it came under siege eleven times, and was taken by the Scots on seven occasions. Wark Castle was the border home of the beautiful Countess of Salisbury, and it may have been during a ball at Wark that Edward III picked up her garter from the floor and uttered the immortal words: '*Honi soit qui mal y pense*'. According to another story, Edward's conduct was far less honourable when on a visit to the beautiful countess in 1342, he subjected her to a particularly brutal rape – his obsession taking his attention away from the siege of Calais.

Etal Castle (Landranger 74 9239) was built during 1341–5 by Sir Robert de Manners. Much of it was destroyed by James IV when he invaded

England in 1496, in support of the pretender, Perkin Warbeck. Despite presenting a ruinous aspect, it has a well preserved keep and gatehouse.

Ford Castle (Landranger 74 9437), is thirteenth century in origin, having been built by Odinel de Ford. His daughter married Sir William Heron, who transformed it into a courtyard castle with four towers. James IV made his headquarters here before the Battle of Flodden and it is said that he lingered rather longer than was advisable because of the beauty of Lady Heron, whose husband was then James's prisoner. The room occupied by the Scottish king, complete with secret staircase, still exists. Having taken a further severe battering from the Scots in 1549, Ford was rebuilt in the form of an Elizabethan fortified manor. Held by the Royalists from the outbreak of the Civil War, it was taken by the Scots for the last time in 1644.

The border country is, indeed, a paradise for anyone with an interest in ruined castles, reminders of Northumberland's turbulent past when every man who dwelt on the Tweed had always to have his wits about him and his broadsword at the ready.

# Further Information

In its capacity as one of the best known of English battles, Flodden warrants a chapter in most of the classic books on the subject of British battlefields. Barrett, Burne and Seymour all cover the battle, as do Young and Adair in *From Hastings to Culloden*. Of particular interest is Charles Knightly's *Flodden: The Anglo-Scottish War of 1513*.

Ordnance Survey maps for the area are Landranger 74 and Pathfinder 463.

Motorists may reach the battlefield from the A697 Coldstream–Wooler road. Follow the signposts from the A697, via Branxton.

Rail travellers should make for Berwick-on-Tweed (tel: 0191 232 6262). For details of bus services from Berwick, call 01835 823301. There is no National Express coach link.

Norham and Etal Castles are both English Hertiage properties. Norham may be visited throughout the year, Etal during the summer season only.

# 9
# THE BATTLE OF NEWBURN
## 28 August 1640

## *Introduction*

In addition to his struggle with the English Parliament, Charles I had to contend with his disaffected subjects north of the border. In both cases he sought confrontation resulting in wars which he lost.

The Scottish problem had its roots in the policies of Charles's father, James VI of Scotland and I of England, who viewed the Kirk of Scotland as a threat to royal absolutism. A Church organized from the bottom upwards, through representative bodies to a General Assembly, was far too suggestive of democracy. Accordingly, he introduced a programme of ecclesiastical 'reforms', aimed at ensuring that the Kirk's authority remained subservient to his own. Seizing control of the General Assembly, he used it as a venue for putting his plans into practice. These included the introduction of rites of a disturbingly ceremonial nature, such as kneeling at Communion, observance of the great feasts and, most important, episcopal confirmation which ratified the power of the bishop, whose authority over the clergy at his diocese had been slowly but surely established. Although James had succeeded in implementing his reforms, by a dual policy of persuasion and bullying, there was still strong opposition at grass-roots level, many folk choosing to attend rural services, where the new rules were less rigorously enforced.

When Charles came to the throne, he did nothing to allay the Scots' ever-present fear of a return to 'Popery', stipulating that an Anglican service, conducted by priests attired in appropriate clerical garb, should be introduced at both St Andrews and Holyrood. In 1635 he compounded the 'insult' by introducing a new Prayer Book, the Kirk responding by drafting and issuing what became known as the National Covenant.

Drawn up by a minister, Alexander Henderson, and a lawyer, Archibald Johnson, the Covenant rejected all innovations in favour of a return to the reformed church. The fact that its authors were careful to acknowledge allegiance to the king could not detract from the document's ulterior motive of presenting a direct challenge to Royal authority. Needless to say, Charles refused to consider any response suggestive of compromise, and the growing body of supporters of the Covenant, known as Supplicants, developed the Henderson-Archibald thesis into a revolutionary charter, demanding the withdrawal of the Liturgy and the deposition of the bishops.

Royal declarations to the effect that the Supplicants would be treated as traitors merely spurred them on to greater abominations. Soon, they were speaking openly of a 'free Parliament' as a means of attaining their ends. A leading light of the reform movement was James Graham, Marquis of Montrose, who recognized the importance of presenting a united front. Charles, who was depending on divisions arising between the various factions constituting the Covenanters, authorized his Commissioner in Scotland, the Marquis of Hamilton, to promise a free Parliament provided the Covenant were set aside. Wisely, Montrose argued against taking the king at his word. Subsequently, a General Assembly which met in November 1638 took it upon itself to abolish episcopacy, deposing the bishops and all other clergy who opposed the Covenant – a decision made after Hamilton had dissolved the meeting, and therefore unlawful. In making his report to the king, Hamilton described Montrose as the most 'vainly foolish' activist at the Assembly. It had already been remarked by one astute observer during the tussle that Montrose would not be happy until he was dangling at the end of a rope.

# The Road to Newburn

With both sides in the dispute refusing to give ground, war was inevitable. As far as the king was concerned, the adventure upon which he had set his heart opened up a whole can of worms. In waging war on the non-conformist Scots, it appeared to his European neighbours, embroiled in Protestant–Catholic rivalry, that Charles was displaying a preference for the Spanish camp. And who could tell whither an Anglo-Scottish war would lead – perhaps to the involvement of both countries on opposing sides within a greater continental conflict?

The first campaign mounted by the king, covering the first six months of 1639, demonstrates the hiatus which often existed between a situation as Charles envisaged it, and as it really was in the cold light of day. His plan, requiring 6,000 cavalry and 24,000 infantry, involved making a four-pronged attack. Charles himself would lead the main force across the

General Alexander Leslie. Leslie, a veteran of the Swedish service, was presented to Charles I after his retirement in 1638. Although keen to serve Charles, his first loyalty was to the Covenant. Despite his victory at Newburn, he was created Earl of Leven in 1641. At Marston Moor, his military prowess was less in evidence when he was to be counted among the allied commanders who fled the field (see p. 130). In the final stages of the conflict, Leven's activities were limited largely to siege warfare – his forté. In 1650 he was instrumental in raising an army in support of the future Charles II and, following the Scottish defeat at Dunbar, he was confined to the Tower. Released in 1654, he died in 1661. (Mansell Collection)

border, while Hamilton, in command of the English fleet, landed at Aberdeen. These movements would be supported by assaults launched from Ireland on Dumbarton and Kintire. In the event, he could manage to raise only 20,000 ill-equipped and poorly trained troops, commanded by the Earls of Arundel and Essex.

With the experience of centuries of border raiding behind them, the Scots had no such difficulties. A hard core of professional soldiers had returned from Germany to train recruits and the Scottish forces were under the command of a competent general, Alexander Leslie. On 21 March 1639 the Scots took Edinburgh Castle, followed by Dalkeith and, with it, the Crown Jewels of Scotland. On 23 March Dumbarton Castle was taken without a struggle, as was Aberdeen seven days later. By the time Charles reached York, on 30 March, the war was already lost.

With the leisurely optimism for which he would become famous during the coming decade, the king tarried in York before beginning a casual march northwards. While Charles himself was adequately provided for, his men remained desperately short of food, drink and shelter, yet he seemed blissfully unaware that their morale was at a dangerously low ebb. It was not until the end of May that the Royal party arrived at Berwick.

On 2 June a force of 3,000 infantry supported by 1,000 cavalry was despatched to challenge Leslie's Scots who were approaching Kelso. However, the mere sight of the fierce clansmen proved sufficient to send them running back to camp, and when the Scots appeared on the opposite bank of the River Tweed, Charles was persuaded to call a halt to the campaign.

By the Pacification of Berwick, most of the demands of the Covenanters were met, the king agreeing to a free Assembly and a free Parliament in exchange for the disbanding of the Scottish army and the return of the occupied castles. The Scottish army withdrew and the keys of the castles were duly returned – but Charles, having no intention of recognizing a free Parliament, was merely angling for a second chance to bring matters to a successful conclusion by force of arms.

The 'Short Parliament' of the spring of 1640 failed to vote the money that was needed to mount a more efficient campaign, and the new army duly raised was no better than its predecessor. Similarly, the Scots army of over 20,000 men, reassembled in mid-July near Dumbarton, was just as efficiently led and managed by Leslie as before. On 20 August the Scots crossed the Tweed at Coldstream, while Charles, accompanied by his new Commander-in-Chief, the Earl of Strafford, hurried north to the succour of Newcastle which, they had learned, was in no shape to withstand a Scottish attack.

# The Battle of Newburn

Montrose, who accompanied Leslie, set an example to his men by wading across the Tweed on foot – not that they needed much encouragement to prosecute what they considered to be a Holy War. A token force sent out from Berwick to impede their progress towards Newcastle was brushed aside contemptuously. Arriving at Newburn, 10 miles from his objective, on 27 August, Leslie found a strong force of 3,000 infantry and 1,500 cavalry, which had been sent out from Newcastle, drawn up on the south bank of the river. The Newburn ford – in the spot occupied today by Newburn Bridge – was one of several fording points along the Tyne, but it was the lowest and, after a very wet summer, it was the most practicable place to cross.

In fact, there would have been no need for Leslie to cross the river but, although anxious to push on to Newcastle, he could not risk being taken in the rear should the English decide to cross over to the north bank and follow him in. Therefore, he divided his 20,000 strong army. One division, under Montrose, went on to Newcastle while Leslie remained with the other.

Newburn Bridge. The present-day bridge probably occupies the site of the seventeenth-century ford upon which the Battle of Newburn centred. In the background is the Church of St Michael and All Angels. Leslie positioned makeshift cannon on the old Norman tower.

As darkness fell, Leslie occupied the high ground above the village, concealing his artillery amid the ragged bushes covering the hillside. He had been short of cannon, but had been able to improvise thanks to a stratagem he had learned in Germany, which involved the manufacture of small calibre temporary cannon. Capable of firing only a few rounds before bursting, they could still help to give the enemy a misleading impression of the extent of one's fire-power. Some guns were also placed on the tower of the old Norman church. Lord Conway, commanding the English force, had set up batteries of his own on hastily thrown-up breastworks on the level land stretching along the south bank, in addition to occupying the higher land towards Ryton.

During the morning of 28 August the armies faced one another, neither seemingly anxious to make the first move. According to tradition, the fighting was started by a single foolhardly Scot who galloped forward. In an alternative scenario, the Scot merely cantered up to the river to water his horse. Unsportingly, he was shot dead. In the artillery exchanges which followed, the English came off worst, their undisciplined gun crews, overawed at the apparently superior fire-power of the Scots, began to abandon their positions.

Recognizing that this could be the right time to attempt a crossing,

Leslie sent up a detachment of cavalry to test the water. The English forward gun positions having been abandoned, the small party crossed without undue difficulty, giving Leslie sufficient confidence to start sending over his infantry. At this juncture, the English cavalry, led by a young Henry Wilmot – at the beginning of a distinguished career – might have been expected to enter the fray, but the thunder of Leslie's guns threw them into disarray.

A perennial problem with interpreting the course of battles is that detailed contemporary accounts – where they exist – are sometimes very partisan, reflecting the loyalties of the chroniclers, and English accounts of Newburn do tend to tone down the extent of the panic within the English ranks. However, despite any resistance which may have been shown by individuals, there is little doubt that Conway's men were soon in full flight. Wilmot, marooned on the level ground between the river and the advancing Scots, was captured.

Leslie may have been unable to mount an organized pursuit of the English because of the rising tide which rendered the river no longer fordable. With a portion of his force stranded on the north bank, he must have been concerned lest Conway should return. But such fears were groundless, for the English did not stop running until they reached Newcastle.

## The Aftermath

The English refusal to fight meant that casualties on both sides were light, with only a few dozen dead. Conway, accused of cowardice, threw the blame on his recruits whom he described as 'the meanest sort of men about London' – which was probably true. Some weeks before, Sir Jacob Astley had only half-jokingly commented that he was 'ready to receive all the arch-knaves of this Kingdom and arm them . . . '.

Charles retreated to York, where a greater effort was made to knock his rabble army into shape. Still entertaining hopes of a victory, the king awaited an Irish landing on the west coast of Scotland – an integral part of his original master plan. Meanwhile, Leslie, approaching Newcastle, was unable to believe his luck when he discovered that the English garrison had abandoned the city. Initially the Scots, welcomed by the populace, behaved remarkably well and the border folk, who had been expecting an orgy of rape and pillage, made no great fuss.

In addition to coping with the Scottish problem, Charles was also having to deal with the increasingly awkward Parliamentary opposition headed by John Pym. To the usual complaint about ship-money were added expressions of horror at the prospect of an Irish Catholic army on the mainland. On the verge of having to call another Parliament, Charles's response was to call a Council of Peers at York in order to whip up support.

By the time the Council met on 24 September, it was clear that, for logistical reasons, the hoped-for Irish intervention was not going to be forthcoming. Also, Edinburgh and Carlaverock Castles – the latter strategically sited on the Solway Firth – had both fallen to the Scots. In view of these set-backs, the king had to take a conciliatory line, agreeing both to call a Parliament and to set up a commission to discuss peace terms with the Scots. In the negotiations which took place at Ripon, the English were forced to accept humiliating terms, including, as an interim measure, Scottish occupation of the six northern counties – being paid £860 per day for the privilege.

The 'Long Parliament', of November 1640–March 1641, ratified the Ripon discussions, sending the Scots home £200,000 richer. And yet, in his opening speech on 3 November, Charles twice made reference to the Scots as rebels, adding that money should be voted to keep the English army in existence. The move towards conciliation had, after all, been only a feint – yet another attempt to gain time. The king was still looking forward to the day when, with his forces regrouped a second time, he could inflict a lasting defeat on the people with whom his own representatives had just concluded what everyone hoped would be a lasting peace. The Royal attitude was all the more disturbing because Charles had personally arranged for the Scottish Commissioner to meet with Parliament for discussion of the peace terms.

The prime purpose of the Parliament, as far as John Pym and his supporters were concerned, was to impeach the Earl of Strafford. Everyone knew that Strafford had tried to make arrangements to land an Irish army in Scotland. However, evidence was produced to the effect that he had made reference to use of an Irish army 'to reduce this Kingdom'. Pym argued that Strafford had been referring not to Scotland, but to England. The claim was based upon a note found among the papers of the Secretary of State, Sir Harry Vane – an enemy of Strafford, who was only too happy to give evidence. It was one of Vane's tasks to make notes at Council meetings. At one such meeting, Vane had noted that Strafford had used this ambivalent phrase. A slow writer, the Secretary found it difficult to take minutes, and it is possible that he exercised some poetic licence in the discharge of his duties. The accusation may have been absurd, but it was enough to lead Strafford to the block.

If the king had succeeded in subduing the Scots, events might have taken quite a different turn. To what extent, one wonders, was Strafford's fate and, ultimately, that of his master, determined by the outcome of a seemingly insignificant skirmish at a village on the Tyne on 28 August 1640?

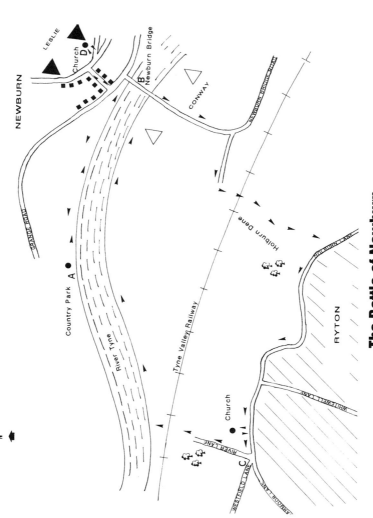

**The Battle of Newburn
26 August 1640**

NEWBURN

LESLIE

Church

D

GRANGE ROAD

Newburn Bridge

B

CONWAY

Country Park A

River Tyne

Tyne Valley Railway

Holburn Dene

Newburn Bridge Road

RYTON

Church

WHITEWELL LANE

RIVER LANE

WESTFIELD LANE

ARMOOR LANE

C

N

# The Walk

**Distance:** 4 miles (6.4 km)

Begin at the Tyne Riverside Country Park (point A; Pathfinder 548 158655). The park was created in the early 1980s, replacing derelict mine workings, scrapyards and rubbish tips. Apart from transforming a particularly depressing section of the River Tyne, the project – albeit incidentally – has facilitated the exploration of this fascinating little battlefield.

From the country park, take the riverside footpath towards Newburn Bridge. If the account of Leslie's use of Newburn church tower is accurate, then it is probable that the present-day structure (point B) which is overlooked by the church, is in close proximity to the seventeenth-century fording points.

Cross the bridge to the south bank. The public footpath system of the area has been subject to changes of direction and, while extensions to the system are always laudable, adequate signposting – absent here – is necessary. Thus, the stranger, impressively kitted out in all-weather rambling gear, struggles to find his bearings and is outpaced by housewives (handicapped by perambulators and heavy shopping) who have a good working knowledge of the local geography.

Immediately beyond the factory site, just before the road bends to the left, is a footpath off to the right (Pathfinder 548 164648). Take this path, bearing to the left, up towards Holburn Dene. With care, negotiate the unmanned railway crossing and bear to the left to walk up the narrow road skirting Holburn Dene – a steep climb, undertaken by the retreating Royalists. (Half-way to the top on the right, the vista opens out into an attractive grassy meadow.)

Emerging on to Holburn Lane, turn to the right and follow the road skirting the northern perimeter of Ryton. Continue walking past the Ryton Park Hotel and on past the village green (where a pause for refreshment at the Jolly Fellows Inn may be in order) to the track leading to the thirteenth-century church. In the northern portion of the churchyard is a mound which may have been utilized by Conway as a vantage point for his artillery.

Walk back to the road and up to River Lane (point C). Walk down towards the Tyne, along the path which remains when River Lane peters out. Cross the railway line once more, to reach the riverbank. At this point, the landscape appears very much as it must have been at the time of the battle. Walk back along the riverside path to the bridge.

Cross the bridge into Station Road, bearing left before turning sharp right to walk up into the High Street. Turn right into the High Street. Just off the

High Street, in Church Bank, stands the Church of St Michael and All Angels (point D). It is usually kept locked because of the risk of vandalism but, as in all cases, there are clear instructions for obtaining the key. The church is worth seeing for the mosaic floor alone, and also for the fine brass lectern. The tower as it appears in the present-day hardly appears to be capable of accommodating very much in the way of artillery.

Leaving the church, return to the bridge, turning to the right in order to follow the path back to the country park.

# Further Explorations

To the south-west of Newburn on the south bank of the Tyne are the remains of Prudhoe Castle (Pathfinder 548 092634). Norman in origin, it became one of the strongholds of the Percy family. The rectangular keep is one of the smallest in England, a dubious distinction redressed by the structure's 10 ft thick and 65 ft high walls.

To the north-west is the village of Heddon-on-the-Wall (Pathfinder 548 134669), indicating, quite correctly, that here is another opportunity to explore Hadrian's Wall – a 280 yd stretch up to 10 ft in thickness. The village itself occupies the site of a milecastle. The hill due north of Heddon, marked on the map (Pathfinder 548 141694) as Heddon Law is a site of some antiquity. As one of the few examples of relatively high ground in the area, it was used by the Scots from time to time on their frequent border raids.

To the east, a 4 mile journey along the A69 will bring one to the centre of Newcastle – with which the rail traveller may already be acquainted. To say that Newcastle's cultural heritage has not suffered from the process of industrialization would not be possible. However, the diligent explorer may still find fragments of masonry that speak of the ancient life of the city.

Newcastle began as a Roman fort on Hadrian's Wall, with the name *Pons Aelli*, as a result of the bridge which Hadrian built over the Tyne early in the second century. In Saxon days, with the establishment of a community of monks, the name changed to Monkschester, finally becoming Newcastle with the construction of the new Norman castle by Robert Curthose, eldest son of William the Conqueror, in 1080. The sandstone keep is remarkably well preserved. Dating from the late 1170s, it is of three storeys, with buttresses at the corners and sides. In the Great Hall, measuring an impressive 30 ft by 10 ft 9 in, John Balliol, the King of Scotland, did homage to Edward I in 1292. Both Charles I and Cromwell stayed at the castle – the former as a prisoner, the latter as Lord Protector. Such was the city's scant regard for its own history – a situation which has since been remedied – that at one stage in the not too distant past, it was proposed to convert the castle keep into a railway signal-box. The railway now separates the keep from the thirteenth-century castle gatehouse, the Black Gate, the main entrance. Although 82 ft high, only the lower portion comprises original work. The castle last saw active service in the '45 Rebellion, when Newcastle served as headquarters for the Hanoverian command.

It was once said that for strength and magnificence, Newcastle's medieval town walls – built during the reigns of Edward I and Edward II – surpassed all others. Once boasting no less than seven main gates and nineteen towers, very little now remains. By the time of the Civil War, the circuit had already fallen into disrepair, and remedial work undertaken by the Royalists to render the town defendable was nullified when several sections were mined by the Scots. However, modern restoration work has preserved a portion of the West Wall, running along Stowell Street together with the Plummer and Sallyport Towers in the East Wall.

Of Norman origins, the Cathedral Church of St Nicholas did not achieve Cathedral status until 1882, and much of its history is of interest to students of the late Victorian era and beyond, but it is worthy of note that Charles I was compelled to attend services here – and, on more than one occasion, he had to listen to the minister's denunciation of his own reign.

# Further Information

The Battle of Newburn has received attention from Barrett in *Battles and Battlefields in England* and also from John Kinross in *The Battlefields of Britain* – although Newburn is curiously absent from Kinross's later, updated volume.

Ordnance Survey maps for the area are Landranger 88 and Pathfinder 548.

Despite its proximity to Newcastle – it is only 4 miles from the city centre – Newburn has retained its individuality, nestling in what is still essentially a semi-rural landscape. It is situated off the A69 and motorists should follow the signposts through the town to the country park.

Mainline Rail terminals are Newcastle (tel: 0191 232 6262) and Carlisle (tel: 01228 44711), linking with the Tyne Valley Line. The nearest station is Blaydon, from where it is a 2 mile walk to Newburn Bridge. Details of bus services between Newcastle and Newburn can be obtained by calling 0191 276 1411. For details of the many National Express coach links with Newcastle, call 0191 261 6077.

Prudhoe Castle, in the care of English Heritage, is open all year, as is the Heddon-on-the-Wall fragment of Hadrian's Wall.

# 10
# THE SIEGE OF YORK
## 21 April to 16 July 1644

## *Introduction*

York's advantageous position had always encouraged settlement. In prehistoric times, settlers were attracted by a major topographical feature – the glacial moraine, providing a well-drained, if comparatively low, causeway across the Vale of York, bridging the gap between east and west. And although the site is over 40 miles from the sea, the River Ouse has always been navigable by sea-going vessels.

The Romans were quick to appreciate its strategic significance in terms of meeting a need to establish a fortress to assist in the northward expansion of the Empire. Due to resistance from the warlike Brigantes, however, it was not until AD 71 that they were able to gain a foothold. From the fort constructed by the Roman Governor Cerialis, for the Ninth Legion, and occupying an area of 50 acres, grew the modern town plan.

*Eboracum*, as it came to be known, was at the centre of a road system. To the north-west lay Catterick, to the south-east, Brough, on the banks of the River Humber. Malton lay to the north-east, while the road south led to Tadcaster and Doncaster before making a gentle arc to Lincoln. The development of a substantial civil settlement was the natural result of the protection afforded by the fort.

At the end of the fourth century, the Roman occupation of Britain ended. The town survived – only to be struck by a natural disaster sometime after AD 450 when severe flooding destroyed the greater portion of the inhabited area on both sides of the river.

An upturn in the decaying settlement's fortunes came two centuries later with the conversion to Christianity of King Edwin, for the small wooden church built by St Paulinus for Edwin's baptism represented an ideal from which York Minster would evolve. It is generally accepted that despite the survival and continued use of many Roman facilities, Edwin's association

Clifford's Tower. Although having suffered from vandalism in the late fifteenth century, Clifford's Tower still presented a daunting sight to the besieging Parliamentarian forces.

with the town marks the end of *Eboracum* and the beginnings of *Eoforwic*. During the Anglian years, overseas trade and some manufacturing activities – metalworking, for example – did develop, but these remained secondary to the main functions of the settlement, which were primarily administrative. *Eoforwic* became a seat of learning and an important royal and ecclesiastical centre. Surviving documentation makes tantalizing references to the establishment of the Minster.

Although little is known of York throughout the period of the Danish supremacy – from AD 866 to 954 – it seems that, like those before and after them, the Danes appreciated its value, encouraging commerce as well as embarking on a rebuilding and development programme of their own. However, the Vikings, who tended to demolish everything they could not understand, had little time for book-learning. Their destruction of what was a priceless library created an intellectual wilderness, and it would be a millennium before York's reputation as a seat of learning was re-established with the foundation of the new university.

By 1066 a street plan not dissimilar to that which exists today had already been established but, with the Norman Conquest, the town once again underwent a severe transformation. Fortifications were the order of the day, and York Castle – of which Clifford's Tower survives – was constructed on the east bank of the Ouse. The damming of the River Foss provided it with a moat. York Minster was rebuilt and St Mary's Abbey was founded. The system of now-famous 'Bars' and outer walls developed in piecemeal fashion during the twelfth and thirteenth centuries.

In the sixteenth century the growing administrative importance of London and the development of the West Yorkshire textile trades led to something of a decline in York's fortunes, yet it still clung tenaciously to its reputation as capital of the north of England. The establishment of the Council of the North – although its real purpose was to secure the north's obedience to the Crown – helped to foster this impression. In fact, the citizens of York needed little in the way of encouragement to make themselves agreeable to the Crown, James I and, later Charles I being' entertained on a lavish scale. However, the time was drawing near when the city's ostensible loyalty would be put to the test. . . .

# The Road to York

As in several major cities, preparations in York for a possible siege during the Civil War had been put in hand well before the event itself occurred. Suburbs had grown up outside the medieval defensive wall and, in the event of attack, the plan was for everyone to retire within the walls, in much the same way that folk from outlying regions would have sought refuge in the distant past. There was still an outer moat, but it was dry in places and used mainly as a convenient dump for household waste. However, there was still deep water in the moat surrounding Clifford's Tower, the keep of the old Norman castle. As both Clifford's Tower and the wall had fallen into considerable disrepair, remedial work was speedily undertaken.

In addition, new defences were constructed outside the walls. Nothing now remains of these 'sconces' or earthworks, both their number and exact locations being uncertain. Perhaps the best known is that which bore the name of The Mount and which stood on high ground on the road which still bears the name – a portion of the present-day A64 to the west of the city.

Finally, efforts were also made to build up adequate stocks of food and ammunition, the York arsenal deriving benefit from Queen Henrietta Maria's mission to the Netherlands. Arriving at Bridlington early in 1643 with much-needed heavy artillery, the queen's route to the Royalist capital of Oxford took her via York, where some of the munitions she had bought from the Dutch were off-loaded.

Although the entry into the War of the Scots and their invasion under Leven culminated in the Siege of York, there were other contributory events happening much nearer home. When Newcastle marched towards the border in response to the Scottish challenge, he appointed John Bellasyse Governor of York (replacing the late Sir William Saville) and Commander-in-Chief of Yorkshire. Bellasyse, who was later to distinguish himself in the Third Siege of Newark, had instructions to assume what Newcastle called 'a defensive posture'. With only 5,000 men comprising mainly infantry under his command, he was hard pressed to hold his ground – a situation that the Roundheads were quick to exploit.

Between 10 and 20 February Sir William Constable led some enterprising raids out of Hull, scoring outstanding successes in skirmishes at Kilham, Bridlington, Driffield and Whitby. With the limited cavalry resources available to him, there was little that Bellasyse could do to stem these guerrilla raids in the East. Instead, he concentrated his attention on the West Riding and, contrary to Newcastle's orders, went on to the offensive.

In fact, under continual pressure from Roundhead forays, he had little choice. On 5 March Colonel John Lambert drove the Royalists from Bradford, punishing them again later in the month when Bellasyse attempted to retake the town. It was a particularly cruel blow because when the Royalists seemed to be on the verge of victory, Lambert had led his exhausted men on a determined charge from their defensive trenches to scatter their assailants.

Bellasyse had set up his field command post at Selby, mid-way between the West Riding and Hull, and it was to Selby that he fell back on receiving the news that Lambert was to be joined by the Fairfaxes, father and son. On 11 April the combined Roundhead forces launched an assault on Selby. Fierce fighting in the narrow, winding streets resulted in a heavy Royalist defeat, leaving the wounded Bellasyse a prisoner, the Royalist army destroyed, and the road to York wide open.

# The Siege of York

Between 21 and 23 April Leven and the Fairfaxes took up their siege positions. Leven set up his headquarters at Middlethorpe, the Scots sealing off York to the west and south, on an arc running from Poppleton to Fulford. Lord Fairfax, operating from Heslington Hall, took responsibility for the east, from Fulford to the Red Tower. To the north, the way remained open. Although this was unsatisfactory, the allied leaders felt that an attempt to encompass the whole of the strongly garrisoned city would have left them over-stretched.

On the inside, Newcastle was trying to cope with the logistics of conservation and rationing of supplies. He had sent away most of his cavalry, which lessened the strain, albeit at the cost of depleting the strength of the garrison. Even so, there were still some 4,000 troops to be fed and housed. The besiegers had no such problems, being billeted in the surrounding villages. The Scots, in particular, helped themselves to anything they lacked.

For the first few weeks of the siege, until the appearance of the Earl of Manchester on 4 June, fighting was sporadic. His arrival meant that the gap to the north could now be plugged. In addition, a battery was erected upon Lamel Hill, from which the city defences could be bombarded. As a result, Clifford's Tower suffered some damage and the approach to Walmgate came under allied control. Fairfax's engineers managed to mine Walmgate Bar, but the subterfuge was discovered in time, the defenders being able to render the mines harmless.

The suburbs outside the walls in all directions were destroyed, most of the damage being inflicted by the garrison. As the cordon around the city was drawn tighter, so the defenders retreated within the walls, setting fire to everything outside as they did so – a potentially dangerous ploy because the burnt-out shells of the once prosperous homes could be used as cover. This had happened at Newark and history repeated itself here, with allied snipers making full use of the facility.

Only too conscious of the overwhelming strength of the investing forces, Newcastle's strategy was to play for time, in the expectation that, in the best tradition, Prince Rupert and his cavalry would soon come galloping to the rescue. By offering to parley with the allies, he was able to gain a valuable week. Following the collapse of negotiations, which had comprised a gentlemanly exchange of letters between Newcastle and the allied leaders, there was a concerted effort to break into the city.

Among the 'weak points' identified for the exercise was St Mary's Tower – which was to be mined – and the Manor, which had been the home of the late Earl of Strafford in his capacity as Lord President of the Council of the North. This may have constituted part of an overall strategy for storming the walls at several points simultaneously, but it seems that the assault on the north-west corner was undertaken prematurely. According to some contemporary reports, a Colonel Crawford, anxious to win for himself the glory of taking the city, took it upon himself to spring the mines under St Mary's and storm the breach with 300 men. On 16 June the tower was blown up and the Manor taken but, unable to keep up the assault, the small force was cut off, sustaining heavy casualties.

The truth of the matter may well be that communications between the three allied commanders left something to be desired and that Crawford was made the scapegoat. Some townsfolk must have been killed or injured in the tower explosion and precious manuscripts – records appertaining to the great religious houses of the north – stored there were destroyed.

In fact, the garrison seems to have been standing up to the siege comparatively well. Although the 'spotted fever' was in evidence, many of the besiegers – particularly the Scots – had also fallen ill. Fairfax complained that he was running short of firearms and ammunition and that his men were owed four months' back pay. (The cost of keeping Fairfax's army in the field was in the region of £15,000 per month.) On top of all this, word of Rupert's approach was expected daily.

The circumstances surrounding the prince's arrival and events leading up to the Battle of Marston Moor – described in Chapter 11 – must also have been a time of great anxiety for the garrison. Efforts to break out and get news to Rupert had proved futile, for the net around York had been drawn much tighter than was usual in Civil War siege situations. When the allies marched out to the moor, the townsfolk were left in a state of limbo, knowing that their fate would depend on the result of the coming battle. At least they had the sense to re-provision the city to the best of their ability.

What, then, did they feel when the weary procession of survivors of the beaten Royalist army appeared at Micklegate Bar on the evening of 2 July? For a time, it was feared that Rupert himself had been killed or captured, for he did not arrive until eleven o'clock.

The allies were slow in resuming the siege, thereby giving Rupert the opportunity to regroup and march out. (Newcastle left for Scarborough and thence, by ship, for Hamburg.) When they did return, on 4 July, the allies were determined to bring matters to a speedy conclusion. Fresh batteries were set up and by 11 July, when they were in a position to mount an all-out assault, they gave the garrison one final opportunity to capitulate. The offer was accepted for, with Rupert's army beaten, there could be no hope of relief.

The surrender was negotiated by Sir Thomas Fairfax, who did much to ensure that it was honourable. The remnant of the garrison was permitted to march out, unmolested, the townsfolk were to be allowed to resume their pre-siege activities in whatever remained of their homes, and there was to be no further damage inflicted on any buildings – a measure designed to protect the churches.

On 16 July the garrison surrendered on these very favourable terms. The Siege of York, which had lasted for five days short of three months, was over.

# The Aftermath

With the cessation of hostilities in the area, York was no longer a battleground, but the struggle was far from over. Although, for the moment, Parliament held the north firmly in its grasp, there was no guarantee that a lasting peace had returned to the region. The following year, for example, the brilliant success of Montrose's Scottish campaign made Charles consider marching north to join him. And, for a time, with Fairfax and Leven poised to stop him, it looked as though Yorkshire could be the scene of another major battle. And so, the process of rehabilitation was tempered by the need to maintain adequate defences and much of the immediate work undertaken to restore the fabric of the city concentrated on repairs to its outer walls.

Naturally, officials with Royalist sympathies were replaced by supporters of the Parliamentary cause, whose duties involved translating Parliamentary policy into practice. These included the payment and billeting of a reduced garrison of 100 soldiers.

York's status as a cathedral city meant that there was certain to be some conflict on ecclesiastical matters. The terms of surrender had made no reference to freedom of worship. Perhaps people presumed – mistakenly – that it was covered by the clauses referring to citizens being able to enjoy all former privileges and the prohibition of defacement and looting of buildings. Following the surrender of the city, Parliamentarian troops had participated in a service of thanksgiving in the Minster and, thereafter, the ceremonial element in all services was severely curtailed. Sunday attendance, however, was made compulsory on pain of fine or imprisonment. Much church property was confiscated and either destroyed or sold. Four puritan ministers, including Edward Bowles, were appointed to preach in the Minster. Each was provided with a house formerly belonging to a prominent Royalist.

Royalists or folk who were unfortunate enough to be caught in York at the commencement of the siege were heavily fined. Francis Danby of South Cave (near Hull) was fined £320 for serving as a major of a troop of horse in Newcastle's army. Walter Hawkesworth was fined £240 for merely taking refuge within the city walls. John Story, an infirm octogenarian, was fined £50 because his son fought on the Royalist side. And one Francis Nevile was fined £2,000, presumably because he could afford to pay it.

Despite these measures, there still remained within the city a strong Royalist lobby, ready to respond to a call to action. In the wake of the final defeat at Worcester in 1651, a countrywide hardcore of committed Royalists known as the Sealed Knot was formed, the conspirators plotting a coordinated uprising for the spring of 1655. However, Parliament was kept informed through its network of spies, and on 8 March dispersed an armed gathering on Marston Moor.

York was still occupying centre stage on the eve of the Restoration when the army and Parliament were bickering over how to solve the problems created by Cromwell's death. George Monck, the army commander in Scotland, resented the eminence of the English generals, Lambert and Fleetwood. If Monck were to successfully challenge his colleagues, it was important for him to gain control of York. Aided and advised by Sir Thomas Fairfax, he achieved his aim, and his entry to the city may be regarded as the first step towards the Restoration of the monarchy.

## *The Walk*

**Distance:** 3½ miles (5.63 km)

The walk, which is based on a perambulation of the city walls, can be started at any of the Bars. For travellers by road, Fishergate Bar is a good starting-point because of its proximity to the long-stay car parking facility in Kent Street.

Fishergate Postern (point A; Pathfinder 665 607513), fifteenth century in origin, is an isolated, seemingly neglected structure, strangely at odds with its surroundings. Its medieval origins are apparent to the casual observer as it is the only one of the surviving smaller gateways to remain unaltered.

The east-bound section of the wall is easily reached by stone steps which lead to what is a surprisingly narrow walk-way. However, the drop on the inner side is not severe. It is no longer possible to walk through the Bars. On reaching Walmgate Bar, therefore, walk down to the road to rejoin the wall on the other side. This south-east corner suffered much damage during the siege. All the houses outside the wall, well into the present-day Lawrence Street, were destroyed and Walmgate Bar itself had to be substantially rebuilt in 1648.

To the left, incongruous amid modern blocks of flats, is St Margaret's Church (point B). Young and fit walkers can slip down from the wall at this point, while the more staid will have to descend from the Red Tower, ahead, and walk back. St Margaret's, now closed and in a ruinous state, is of interest because of its porch. Belonging originally to St Lawrence's Church, which was badly damaged during the siege, the porch was preserved by Sir Thomas Fairfax and afterwards removed to St Margaret's. Return to the wall – and to the Red Tower (point C). The red-brick edifice was built towards the end of the fifteenth century for use as a watch tower and, again, suffered through bombardment.

The Red Tower marks the beginning of a gap in the wall. The tower itself stood at what was once the southern tip of an area of marshland known as the King's Fishpond, an expanse of water which had been formed when the River Foss had been dammed during the construction of York Castle. By the date of the siege, had it not been on the verge of drying up, it would have constituted an effective barrier as far as any aggressors were concerned.

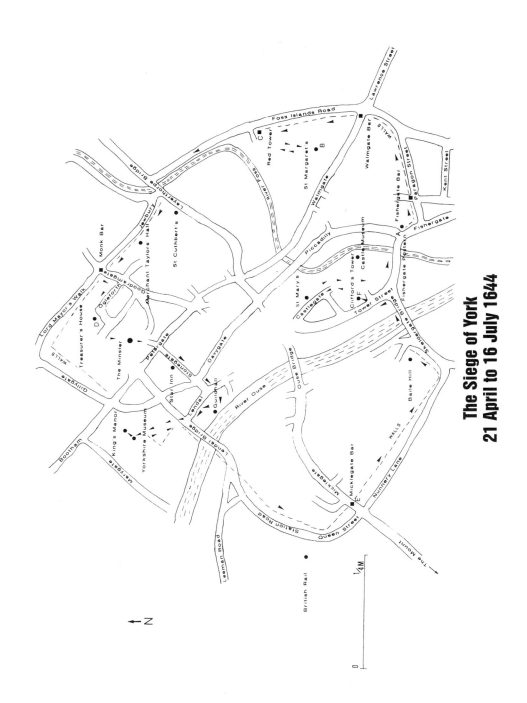

**The Siege of York
21 April to 16 July 1644**

Continue along Foss Islands Road, crossing the river by Layerthorpe Bridge to rejoin the wall in Jewbury. A formidable postern was sited here until its demolition in 1829. On the left is St Cuthbert's Church, stranded in a sea of later development and looking as forlorn as St Margaret's. Finding a twentieth-century role for these medieval places of worship is a great problem. A little further along is Merchant Taylor's Hall – one of many buildings used to provide temporary hospital facilities for the wounded.

At Monk Bar, descend and walk into Goodramgate. A right turn into Ogleforth will bring one to the Treasurer's House (point D). Once the residence of the Treasurers of York Minster, it is well known for its ghosts of Roman soldiers, sighted in the cellar by a young plumber's apprentice in 1953.

A walk into Minster Yard offers an opportunity to take a coffee break and a few moments to admire the exterior of one of the medieval mason's most outstanding achievements. Although the Minster was not a military objective, it is still surprising that it survived unscathed. It must have been a great temptation for the defenders to take advantage of its elevation by mounting guns on the top. Several well bred casualties of both the siege and Marston Moor were buried in the Minster, and the Chapter House contains a memorial to the Fairfaxes for using their influence to preserve the Minster from destruction after the surrender.

Walk out of the Minster grounds, across Petergate and into Stonegate and the bustle of the city centre – a world apart from the serenity of the walls. In Stonegate is the Star Inn, another building used as a temporary hospital and still reputedly haunted by the cries of the wounded. (York appears to be a ghost hunter's paradise, for boards publicizing various ghost walks are to be found at frequent intervals.)

At the end of Stonegate, at the far side of St Helens Square, is The Guildhall. Severely damaged by an air raid in 1942, it was restored in 1960, the east window being redesigned to include a scene depicting the siege.

From The Guildhall, a short walk up Lendal and across Museum Street leads one into the Museum Gardens and the Yorkshire museum, which has on display a model of the Battle of Marston Moor. In the grounds behind the museum is the King's Manor, the residence of both the Earl of Strafford and, when he visited York, Charles I.

Return to Museum Street and turn to the right, to cross the River Ouse by Lendal Bridge, rejoining the wall at Lendal Tower. The railway station is on the right as one walks around to Micklegate Bar (point E), adorned over the years by many famous heads. (A 'lost' tower – Sadler Tower – destroyed by Roundhead cannon fire, may have occupied the extreme south-west corner of the wall.) It was at Micklegate that the beaten Royalists pleaded for admission after Marston Moor, while those inside attempted to bar the entry of anyone who had not been a member of the original garrison. From

Micklegate, amid the nineteenth-century urban sprawl, one can just make out the rise of the land towards the site of the Royalist gun emplacements on The Mount Sconce.

Continue to Baile Hill. This is perhaps the most attractive portion of the walled walk. Note the steep incline to the moat. (The scars of artillery fire can still be identified along this and other sections of wall.) The tree-covered mound is all that remains of the 'companion' castle to Clifford's Tower. During the siege it was crowned with two cannon. For the last time, descend from the wall, recrossing the Ouse via Skeldergate Bridge. Clifford's Tower (point F) looms up on the left, in Tower Street. Still very defensible in the mid-seventeenth century, new floors and a gun platform were added. In

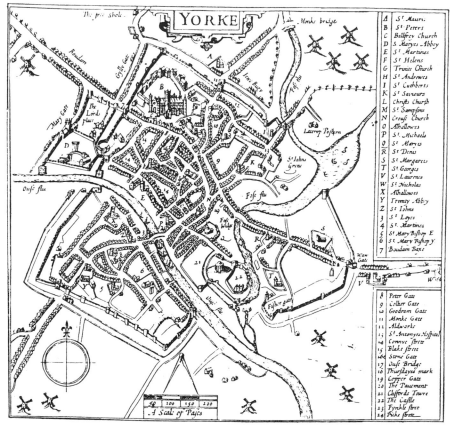

John Speed's map of seventeenth-century York. Note the position of the 'King's Fishpond', forming a 'natural' barrier between the Red Tower and Layerthorpe Postern. Also clearly indicated are St Margaret's Church, St Cuthbert's and St Mary's – all within a street plan not markedly different from that of today.

Castlegate, to the rear of Clifford's Tower, is St Mary's Church, a heritage centre tracing the development of York, including its role in the Civil War.

By retracing one's steps down Tower Street, one arrives back in Fishergate, near the starting-point of the walk.

## Further Explorations

York 'within' the walls is so compact that one is easily seduced into believing that it is possible to sample everything of historical interest in one day. With 2,000 years of recorded history to take into consideration, this is a grave error, as many a visitor has discovered to his or her cost. Another potential pitfall concerns the attention given to Roman York and, in recent years, Viking York. Although the significance of the developmental work in both spheres is not to be decried, there is, none the less, a tendency for it to overshadow less fashionable, though important associations.

The city's best known tourist attraction, undoubtedly, is the Jorvik Viking Centre, a reconstruction of life in tenth-century Jorvik on the site of extensive excavations beneath Coppergate. A street with the people, their dwellings and even the sounds and the smells of the Viking community has been recreated. (This is not an entirely new concept. Many years ago, the Castle Museum, as visitors will know, developed its full-scale reconstructions of Victorian cobbled streets.)

Visitors who arrive by rail may be forgiven for failing to recognize York's past importance as a railway town. As the home of George Hudson, the 'Railway King', it was at the very heart of railway development throughout the 1830s and 1840s. Originally a draper's apprentice, Hudson recognized the potential profit which lay in the amalgamation of the hundreds of localized companies which were springing up. His activities in this respect were so successful that, by 1849, he controlled a quarter of the total track mileage in the country. He took a fine house at No. 44 Monkgate, and, later, a country house at Newby Park, complete with its own private railway siding.

At the height of his fame, Hudson was such a powerful figure that he was often referred to as the dictator of York, his employees, family and friends being installed in civic positions which enabled them to look out for the great entrepreneur's interests. He even had a street – Hudson Street – named after him. Following his fall from grace after evidence of financial mismanagement came to light, the name was changed to Railway Street. However, in recognition of the debt owed to him by the city, the original name has since been restored. During the Second World War thousands of 'necessary' train journeys through York were made by new recruits travelling north for training at Catterick and Strensall. The National Railway Museum, to the rear of York station on Leeman Road, is one of the world's largest.

And how many casual visitors to York, one wonders, are aware of the 'Mystery Plays'? That a city which has so long been a centre of religious activity should have a tradition of religious drama is not surprising. The tradition of Craft Guilds performing a Cycle of Plays – forty-eight in number – began in the fourteenth century. Performances took place in the streets on a single day, Corpus Christi Day, beginning at 4.30 a.m. and ending at dusk.

Features with an historical interest for the tourist are manifold. However, no visit to York would be complete without a visit to the Archaeological Resource Centre in St Saviourgate, where one may handle 'finds' and sample ancient crafts.

The connection of Richard III with York is rather a tenuous one. Richard's favourite home in the north was Middleham Castle, yet he did contribute to the survival of the city as the centre of northern government by experimenting with an idea which, under the auspices of Henry VIII, was developed into the permanent Council of the North. Therefore, a visit to the Richard III Museum in Stonegate should be included in any expanded itinerary.

# Further Information

*Sieges of the Great Civil War 1642–1646* by Peter Young and Wilfrid Emberton contains a chapter on the Siege of York – a particularly useful book in that the circumstances of the major sieges, countrywide, can be compared and contrasted. However, indispensable reading is provided by Peter Wenham's classic *The Great and Close Siege of York 1644*.

Ordnance Survey maps for the area are Landranger 105 and, unfortunately, no less than four Pathfinder maps (664, 665, 673 and 674), although a locally purchased street map is of more value.

By road, York is best approached via the A1, along the A59 turn-off from the north, or by the A64 Tadcaster road if approaching from the south. For details of British Rail services, call 01904 642155. For details of National Express coach links, call 01532 460011.

For details of the varying, seasonally regulated opening hours of the buildings referred to in the suggested walk, it is best to contact the Tourist Information Office in York (tel: 01904 621756).

# 11
# THE BATTLE OF MARSTON MOOR
## 2 July 1644

## *Introduction*

The first major battle of the English Civil War was fought at Edgehill on 23 October 1642, an indecisive outcome suggesting that the conflict was likely to be more prolonged than anyone had at first envisaged. In an effort to tip the scales in their favour, each side made overtures to the Scots.

Even when at their most rebellious during the recent Anglo-Scottish Wars, the Scots had always been anxious to assert their allegiance to the monarchy, and, despite the rantings of the Covenanters, there was still a strong Royalist voice striving to be heard. Therefore, despite the common ground of non-conformity between Covenanters and Puritans, it was far from certain that the Scots would come into the war on the side of Parliament. Indeed, there was no guarantee that they would enter the war at all.

For his part, Charles felt that he had done enough to guarantee Scottish support for himself. By appointing his enemies – the Earl of Argyll and Sir Thomas Hope among them – to influential posts, he hoped to win their trust. In theory, appeasement should have worked, as it had in the past – notably during the Wars of the Roses. Instead, it succeeded only in giving the Covenanters power over their own future and in arousing the hostility of the Royalists, who felt that their loyalty had gone unrewarded. Particularly irksome was General Leslie's elevation to a peerage – he became Earl of Leven.

In the end, it was events in Ireland which decided the issue. The Earl of Strafford's arrangements to use an Irish army against the Scots had brought about his fall from grace. Yet, amid the alarm at the possibility of Catholicism being forced on the nation, it was often forgotten – by both Crown and Parliament – that Irish Catholics entertained similar fears of Protestantism being rigidly enforced in Ireland. In the autumn of 1641 the animosity between Protestants and Catholics exploded into an uprising in which Ulster Protestants, most of whom were of Scottish Lowlands extraction, were massacred. The king was enjoying a round of golf when the news was given to him. He went on with his game. The cunning Pym, however, stimulated rumours that Charles had secretly encouraged the rebellious Catholics. It was, said Pym, part of a sinister Popish conspiracy, in which Irish Catholics, the Spanish and the king were all embroiled.

A General Assembly which met in August 1643 came down firmly on the side of Parliament, with which a treaty entitled 'The Solemn League and Covenant' was concluded – the terms of the pact providing for the preservation of the reformed religion in both England and Ireland and for the extermination of Roman Catholicism.

Charles has often been criticized for his handling of the Scottish problem, but it is doubtful whether he could have done anything which would have won him official Scottish backing. In particular, he had no idea who, among his so-called friends, could be trusted. In the Second Scottish Campaign, for example, the loyalties of both Hamilton and Montrose had been divided – for no other reason than adherence to the understandable human impulse to be on the winning side. Hamilton had played an especially difficult game. Certain that the king could not win the war, he had yet to convey an impression of doing his best to achieve victory. His procrastination had kept the Irish army immobile in Ulster. As for Montrose, while active for the Covenantors he had written to Charles, assuring him of his loyalty, obedience and readiness to serve him.

The time was fast approaching when all who had been swept back and forth on the tide of revolution would have to choose sides. Montrose, who was becoming disillusioned with the Covenanters, decided to give his allegiance to the king, warning him, towards the end of 1643, that a Scottish army would be sent over the border in support of the Parliamentary cause.

# *The Road to Marston Moor*

A key date for all concerned was 19 January 1644 for, on that day, a Scottish army crossed the Tweed to make war on the Royalists. It consisted of some 21,000 men – 18,000 infantry and 3,000 cavalry – and was commanded by Alexander Leslie. In 1641 the victor of Newburn had promised never again to bear arms against the king. As always, however, in the hope of absolving themselves from charges of treason, the Scots were keen to point out that they were seeking only to deliver His Majesty from unprincipled advisers who sought to mislead him. After all, had not the terms of the agreement with the English Parliament included a statement to the effect that the Scots sought to maintain His Majesty's authority in preserving the 'true' religion?

With thirty years' experience in continental warfare behind him, the Earl of Leven, as Leslie must now be called, ranked as one of the most experienced commanders in the field. He was a great disciplinarian, a circumstance which fitted in well with the rules and regulations which governed his crusading army. 'Camp followers', in plentiful supply in Royalist baggage trains, were discouraged, morning and evening prayer was compulsory and, oddly enough, irreverent speech against the king was regarded as treason. One wonders how the Scots would have squared a situation in which a Scotsman killed the king – who was not averse to exposing himself to personal danger – on the battlefield.

Leven's march south put a whole new complexion on the war. To date, the action had gravitated towards the south and the west. Now, with a theatre of operations in the north opening up, the Royalists had to review their strategy.

The Marquis of Newcastle, en route to take part in a pincer movement on London, had to confine his attention to this new threat, barely making it back to Newcastle itself in sufficient time to bolster the town defences. Hampered by an especially hard winter of heavy snow and flooding, Leven was unable to make much headway and a stand-off situation developed.

Elsewhere, there was more activity. Charles had hoped to counterbalance the threat from Scotland by recruiting Irish Catholic troops for the Royalist cause. At length only English soldiers, released from service in Ireland, arrived on the scene, to be beaten decisively by Fairfax at Nantwich. Apart from one success when Prince Rupert lifted the siege of Newark, the Royalist gloom continued with a defeat at Cheriton on 29 March. And the no longer snowbound Scots were able to mount an offensive against the Marquis of Newcastle which drove him southwards as far as York, where he remained boxed in by the combined armies of Leven and the Fairfaxes.

The task of relieving York fell, as might be expected, to Rupert, whose progress from Shrewsbury, where he was engaged in training and recruitment, was necessarily slow, for initially he could call on only 8,000 troops. Building up his force en route he enjoyed some success in Lancashire, subduing, in turn, Stockport, Bolton and Liverpool. However, on 3 June the Earl of Manchester had arrived with a third army to join the siege of York – swelling the allied total to 27,000 – and, with still only 17,500 men, Rupert remained at a serious disadvantage.

As far as the prince was concerned, speed was of the essence for, in the south, General Waller was putting Charles under extreme pressure. Rupert's brief – a demanding one – was to relieve York and then march south to relieve the king. What he could not know, as he approached Knaresborough on 30 June, was that the day before, the Royalists had trounced Waller at Cropredy Bridge, giving Charles a valuable breathing space.

Hoping to prevent Rupert from joining Newcastle, the allied commanders

Cromwell's Plump. From this vantage point, Cromwell and the allied generals surveyed the site of the impending Battle of Marston Moor.

decided to abandon the siege (and, with it, all their equipment) and set out for Marston Moor, an expanse of heath to the west of York, commanding the approach roads from Knaresborough. However, while undoubtedly a sound manoeuvre, it failed to take account of the prince's ingenuity. In one of the war's most outstanding pieces of generalship, on 1 July Rupert struck out for Boroughbridge, where he crossed the Ouse. Continuing north-east, he negotiated the Swale at Thornton Bridge before turning south to join the route of the present-day A19 to York. To cover all eventualities – and to his credit – Manchester had stationed a regiment of dragoons in charge of a bridge of boats at Poppleton, but Rupert swept them aside before making camp in the nearby Forest of Galtres, after a forced march of 22 miles. Newcastle was instructed to have his men ready at dawn the next day in order to face the now discomfited allies on Marston Moor.

# The Battle of Marston Moor

The allies passed an uneasy night on the moor, trying to ponder Rupert's next move. Unaware of his intention to fight and afraid that he might attempt to slip away to join the king, they decided to march to Selby and Cawood (where they had another bridge of boats) in order to block the route to the south. Accordingly, in the morning the main body of the army set off to Tadcaster, leaving 4,000 dragoons behind. When Rupert's forces began arriving on the moor, the allied column was strung out vulnerably, and a determined cavalry assault at this time could have wrought havoc in its ranks.

However, the prince could do nothing until reinforced by Newcastle, who arrived on the scene, in leisurely fashion, at nine o'clock – and without most of his men who had refused to budge until they received arrears in pay. Those who did accompany the marquis were the worse for wear following a night of celebrations occasioned by the lifting of the siege. The remainder, the famous Whitecoats – so named because of their tunics of undyed cloth – eventually appeared in mid-afternoon, by which time the allies had had sufficient time to regroup.

The Royalist army was drawn up to the north of Marston Lane – the Tockwith–Long Marston road – and the combined Parliamentarian forces to the south. The most prominent feature of the battlefield was a ditch immediately in front of the Royalist lines. Connecting the Syke Beck with the Atterwith Dyke, it was of varying depth, and very probably dry. And in front of it, on the Marston Lane side, was a continuous brushwood hedge.

Under his command Rupert had 11,000 infantry and 6,000 cavalry, together with sixteen pieces of artillery. His right wing, under Lord Byron, comprised 2,600 cavalry and 500 musketeers, and was almost equally balanced by the left wing, with Lord Goring commanding 2,100 horse and 500 musketeers. The centre, under Eythin, consisted of 10,000 infantry, a single brigade of horse and was fronted by musketeers. As Commander-in-Chief, Rupert held in reserve about 650 cavalry. Eythin expressed his disapproval of the overall deployment, advising Rupert that although it looked fine on paper, there was little to commend it in practice. In particular, he felt that the Royalists were far too close to the ditch.

Across the road, the allied army, 28,000 strong, still possessed a strong advantage. Sir Thomas Fairfax, on the right, faced Goring, with Cromwell on the allied left drawn up against Byron. Exact deployment in numerical terms is unclear, but as the allied supremacy was in infantry, it is probable that both sets of wings were evenly matched. The allied centre reflected the conglomerate nature of the force, with three divisions commanded by Manchester, Leven and Lord Fairfax. Twenty-five guns were ranged across Marston Hill, but there appears to have been no reserve.

These manoeuvres having taken up the better part of the day – it was now approaching 7.00 p.m. – Newcastle asked Rupert whether he intended to give battle that night, to which the prince replied that the following morning would be early enough. Rupert went off to his supper, while Newcastle retired to his coach to smoke a pipe.

In the allied lines, there was no such laxity. Gone were the days of chivalry when one waited until one's opponent was ready to fight, for as soon as they perceived the Royalist troops standing down, the Roundhead force began to move forward. According to Sir Thomas Fairfax, it was Cromwell who made first contact. Possibly, the ditch separating the two sides had been filled in at the western end, giving Cromwell a clear run at the opposition. To Rupert's annoyance, Byron immediately launched a countercharge, temporarily checking Cromwell's momentum. Unable to restrain himself, Rupert left his command post in an attempt to bolster the crumbling line, arriving on the scene as Cromwell broke through and the Royalists – including the prince's own regiment – began to fall back in disarray.

The Royalists were also giving ground in the centre. On the left, in particular, Manchester's infantry were making good progress. But for Sir Thomas Fairfax on the right wing, things were not going so well. Like Cromwell, he had tried to slice through the Royalist lines, but had been severely hampered by the hedge and ditch. At the head of 400 horse, he had led a charge which put some of Goring's men to flight. But, instead of halting to regroup, he indulged in a pursuit over the fields towards York. He returned to find that a countercharge by Goring had scattered the bulk of his leaderless force, and it was only by resorting to guile that he was able to regain his own lines.

Having put Sir Thomas's men to flight, Goring's horse swept round on the allied infantry, causing the collapse of the centre right, both Leven and Lord Fairfax joining in the retreat. Leven made for Leeds, Lord Fairfax for his house at Cawood. As soon as he arrived home, Fairfax went to bed. Yet Cromwell and Manchester remained on the field, each very much holding his own.

Cromwell, unlike Fairfax, had kept all his men on the field. Now, in an extraordinary manoeuvre, he led his men around the rear of the Royalist lines to attack Goring's victorious cavalry on the flanks, arriving in the nick of time to save the Scottish regiments of Lieutenant-General Baillie and Major-General Lumsden, which had stood their ground instead of joining in the allied flight. What had appeared to all to be a famous Royalist victory had been turned into a rout. Only Newcastle's Whitecoats refused to surrender, fighting on to near annihilation.

The battle had lasted only two hours, but the fugitives were pursued well into the night, Rupert contriving to evade capture by hiding in a bean field. The Royalist dead numbered over 4,000, Parliamentarian dead possibly as few as 300. That night the allies remained in possession of the field, allowing the defeated Royalists to lick their wounds in York and giving Rupert the opportunity to salvage what he could from the disaster. The following morning, he had succeeded to the extent that he was able to strike out for Lancashire at the head of 6,000 men.

# The Aftermath

Ever since the battle, analysts have wrangled with the question of Rupert's failure in the field. His enemies had marvelled at his apparent invincibility – a reputation which Marston Moor left in tatters. However, the prince had never been an outstanding tactician, and he was ill fitted to take command in a set-piece confrontation on such a huge scale. In skirmishes such as that which occurred at Chalgrove Field (1643), for example, his customary dashing cavalry charge would invariably win the day, whereas at Marston Moor and a year later at Naseby, his preoccupation with one portion of the action had disastrous consequences. Nevertheless, on the evening of 2 July, while his fellow generals wallowed in the misery of defeat, Rupert rallied the remains of his army and marched westward. Although the north was lost, there was still life and hope in the west.

The king was at Evesham when news of the battle reached him. Initial reports suggested that the Royalists had indeed won a famous victory. When it became clear that these were based on mindless optimism as opposed to fact, Charles, with uncharacteristic magnanimity, absolved his nephew of all blame. Rupert's critics suggested that he had acted recklessly by abandoning York to its fate. Yet in withdrawing, he wisely sought to cut his losses and to provide himself with a chance of regrouping in the west and Wales, where there was still much sympathy for the Royal cause.

Meanwhile, in London, Parliament was cock-a-hoop. The end of the war was surely now, at long last, in sight. Far from engendering unity in the Parliamentarian ranks, however, the prospect of total victory served to heighten tension and increase divisions. On the one hand were those who felt that Parliament was now in a sufficiently strong position to open negotiations with the king, with a view to securing an honourable peace settlement. On the other were Cromwell and his supporters who were all for bringing Charles to his knees on the field of battle.

As Cromwell knew, Parliament was far from being in a position of strength, such as would enable it to dictate terms to the king. After all, the Marston Moor victory had owed more to Royalist ineptitude than to Parliamentary generalship. Also, the strategic importance of the north of England had declined since the age of the Wars of the Roses, and the king's withdrawal from the northern counties (only a handful of towns remained to him) meant that while his resources were no longer so over stretched, more Roundhead troops were tied up on garrison duty.

Apart from the promise of a fresh Royalist initiative based on Wales and the west, there were plans, about to bear fruit, for a counter-offensive to be launched from Scotland. At the head of a relatively small, mobile army the

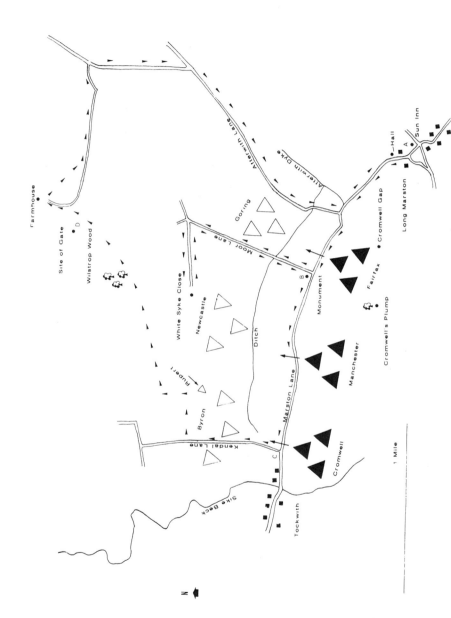

The Battle of Marston Moor
2 July 1644

Farmhouse
Site of Gate
Wilstrop Wood
D
White Syke Close
Newcastle
Rupert
Byron
Kendal Lane
Sike Beck
Tockwith
Cromwell
Manchester
Cromwell's Plump
Fairlax
Long Marston
Cromwell Gap
Sun Inn
Hall
A
Monument
B
Ditch
Marston Lane
Moor Lane
Goring
Atterwith Lane
Atterwith Dyke
C

1 Mile

N

Marquis of Montrose would win a series of dramatic victories which did much to boost morale.

Yet it was not only within the Parliamentarian ranks that Marston Moor created tension. On the Royalist side, there were those who were giving thought to the possible advantages of a cease-fire. In particular, Lieutenant-General Henry Wilmot, one of the best cavalry commanders, perhaps mindful of the serious loss of manpower occasioned by the Royalist defeat, was foolish enough to speak publicly of the wisdom of entering into talks. For his pains, he was arrested in front of his troops, relieved of his command and charged with High Treason – although Charles relented sufficiently to condemn him to exile.

In sum total, therefore, Marston Moor was not viewed by those who participated in it as a decisive battle. While the scales were certainly tipped in favour of Parliament, its failure to press home its advantage was to lead to the Royalists raising their game to a level at which a whole series of match points would be saved.

# The Walk

**Distance:** 9 miles (14.49 km)

A battlefield memorial of such stateliness as that of Marston Moor does tend to attract visitors, and it is unfortunate that nearby off-road car parking is limited to a worn-down grass verge. It is as well, therefore, for motorists – in company with everyone else – to begin in Long Marston village, at the Sun Inn at the corner of Marston Lane (point A; Pathfinder 664 502511).

It is easy to see how Long Marston acquired its name, for houses straggle along Marston Lane to the point of its junction with Atterwith Lane. On the right, a short distance from the junction with the B1224, is Marston Hall, where Cromwell may have slept before or after the battle. At the end of the village on the left is a track leading to Cromwell's Gap (Pathfinder 664 493515), the escape route of many fleeing Royalists. Still a prominent feature of the landscape is Cromwell's Plump (Pathfinder 664 489516), the high point of the land – topped by a tree – to the left. This ridge identifies the preliminary Roundhead positions, to the rear of which was the baggage train.

To the rear of the memorial itself (point B) is a descriptive battle plan, while the memorial itself states (quite firmly) that 'the Parliamentary army, left to the leadership of Oliver Cromwell supported by David Leslie completed the defeat of the forces of Prince Rupert'.

It is still possible to walk down Moor Lane, the track beside the memorial, on the other side of the hedge. The ditch which the Royalists lined can still be made out. Walk up the track which, in wet weather, can be very muddy. It should be remembered that the battle took place in heavy rain and that the heavy-going endured by the present-day rambler would have been experienced to a still greater extent by both cavalry and infantry.

At the fork in the track, turn to the left and continue walking. The field where the track terminates is White Syke Close (Pathfinder 664 487531), where the Whitecoats were all but annihilated, and where they lie buried. One now has to retrace one's steps back to the memorial. It is said that Moor Lane is haunted by the ghosts of exhausted combatants, wearily making their way from the field of battle. And from time to time, as one walks the track, it is difficult to avoid glancing uneasily over one's shoulder.

Turn to the right to continue along Marston Lane, a walk which brings one into Tockwith. During the course of the battle, Cromwell was wounded and he found it necessary to leave the field to have the wound dressed. Cromwell's critics have made much of the fact that while he recovered in a cottage in Tockwith, his Ironsides, under the direction of Leslie, broke Rupert's cavalry. Indeed, a similar situation had arisen at Winceby the previous year when, with Cromwell unhorsed, Fairfax had taken the initiative at the decisive moment. Only much later did historians consider it necessary to enlarge upon Cromwell's admittedly major role in each battle.

In Tockwith, turn right into Kendal Lane (point C). This is the Jorvik Way. Again it is possible to distinguish the line of the old ditch running across the fields. Walk on until reaching the public footpath sign indicating a path to the right (Pathfinder 664 475532), which takes one to the rear of the spot occupied by Rupert's cavalry and the Royalist centre right. If it were possible to continue walking through this field, along the line of the ditch, one would reach the opposite side of White Syke Close. However, the well-marked path turns sharply to the north, before veering north-east to lead one in the direction of Wilstrop Wood. On the western flank of the wood is the site of the bean field where Rupert took refuge. The path continues along the southern edge of the wood and the going – which can be quite heavy in wet weather – becomes a little easier.

At the opposite corner of the wood (point D) there was once a gate, which was the focus of yet another of the many stories which have often been told about the battle. When Rupert's cavalry was in full retreat, galloping by the wood, a young servant girl attempted to facilitate their escape by opening this gate. But the fleeing Royalists, while taking advantage of her forethought, trampled her underfoot, leaving in their wake her poor mangled corpse.

From this point, it would be useful to be able to turn right along the farm track, but according to the Pathfinder 664 Ordnance Survey Map it is necessary to follow the public footpath to Wilstrop Lodge Farm, cross over the ditch and walk back through the field to join the track a little further

White Syke Close. Newcastle's élite 'Whitecoats' made their last stand here. Refusing all invitations to surrender, they were annihilated and lay buried where they fell.

down. At the end, turn right on to the road leading back to Atterwith Lane and Long Marston.

Almost at the junction of Atterwith and Marston Lanes stood a farmhouse (point E) which was the focus of perhaps the most unlikely legend of all connected with the battle. At some indeterminate stage of the fight – presumably during the initial exchanges of artillery fire – the farmer's wife was busily engaged in baking bread when a Royalist cannon-ball entered the house and burst into the oven to destroy the fruits of her labours. As with the story of the girl at the gate, one may express some doubt as to whether country folk, with a major battle raging on their doorsteps, would be going about their daily duties regardless. Of course, there are contemporary tales of solitary rustics who, when questioned by partisans of either side as to their persuasion, denied all knowledge of the conflict which had torn the nation asunder. And often, when the local population were given sufficient notice of an impending battle, instead of taking cover, they would gather at a suitable vantage point to view the proceedings – much as crowds of sightseers congregate at the scene of disasters today, regardless of the dangers involved. So, there may be an element of truth in such stories which are, perhaps, best considered over refreshment at the Sun Inn, to which one may now repair.

# *Further Explorations*

Some 15 miles to the east of Marston Moor, on the road between Harrogate and Ripon, is Ripley Castle (Landranger 99 2861). It has been in the ownership of the Ingilby family since the fourteenth century and is still the family home. At the time of the Civil War, Sir William Ingilby, a committed Royalist, was in residence. Sir William's sister, Jane, fought at Marston Moor disguised as a Royalist trooper. According to tradition, Cromwell spent the night after the battle at Ripley. Sir William having fled following the defeat, Lady Ingilby was alone. She met Cromwell at the door, with a brace of pistols secured in her apron strings, and kept him under surveillance for the whole of what must have been a wretched night. When he left in the morning, Lady Ingilby is reputed to have told him that had he shown the slightest discourtesy, she would have had no hesitation in shooting him dead. Cromwell asked why she needed two pistols, to which she replied that she might have missed with the first.

The east wall of All Saints Church in the village carries the scars of bullets occasioned by the summary execution of Royalists. Buried in the church itself is Sir Thomas Ingilby, the first Ingilby to settle at Ripley. Sir Thomas saved the life of Edward III when the king was attacked by a wild boar while hunting in Knaresborough Forest.

Another church which still bears the marks of bullets is that of Healaugh (Pathfinder 673 498479). A dragoon en route to Marston Moor paused at the village smithy to have a horseshoe replaced, threatening to burn down the blacksmith's house if he did not make haste. The blacksmith replied that he might not get the chance, upon which the dragoon discharged the contents of his carbine at the church door. (Blacksmiths figure prominently in Civil War fables. Invariably, they are presented as morose, taciturn fellows, yet possessing a dry rural wit which invariably leads to the discomfiture of their urban sophisticated protagonists.)

According to some reports, the Battle of Marston Moor had been foretold by the sixteenth-century seer Mother Shipton. Apparently, she gave the location as Bramham Moor, which is only 4 miles away (Landranger 105 4342) and which, to the credulous, is sufficiently close to prove the accuracy of the prediction. In fact, there had been a Battle of Bramham Moor in 1408, the culmination of a revolt by the Earl of Northumberland against the rule of Henry IV. And by a curious coincidence, there was a Civil War skirmish at Bramham on 27 May 1644 – two months prior to Marston Moor – when Royalist-held Bramham Hall fell to Scottish troops.

The village of Nun Monkton, situated 4 miles to the north of Marston Moor, at the confluence of the Ouse and the Nidd (Pathfinder 664 511579) was the home of the Royalist Colonel Sir Henry Slingsby, a participant in both the Siege of York and Marston Moor. During the reign of Stephen, a Benedictine priory was founded here. At the end of the fourteenth century, the Prioress, the young and attractive Margaret Fairfax, presided over fifteen young nuns. A state of affairs developed which led to the launch of an investigation into alleged high-living at the priory. The nuns were found to be draped in furs and jewellery – in addition to being on very intimate terms with the male clergy of the locality. Such tales usually conclude with the bricking up of the culprits. In this case, however, they seem to have escaped with a caution. The nave of the priory survives in the present-day church.

# Further Information

Whereas several battles covered in the present volume are not so well provided for in terms of ready availability of background reading, the same cannot be said of Marston Moor, as all the standard texts contain chapters on the battle. Indeed, the problem revolves around the need for selectivity. However, an effort should be made to read Austin Woolrych's account in his *Battles of the English Civil War*. Leadman's *Battles Fought in Yorkshire* also includes a particularly enjoyable chapter on the battle. Of works devoted specifically to the battle, essential reading is provided by Peter Newman's meticulously researched *The Battle of Marston Moor, 1644* and by Peter Young in *Marston Moor 1644: The Campaign and the Battle*.

Ordnance Survey maps for the area are Landranger 105 and Pathfinder 664.

The village of Long Marston, situated on the B1224, can be approached from the east via York or from the west via Wetherby and the A1. Mainline Rail terminals are York (tel: 01904 642155) and Harrogate (tel: 01532 448133). For details of bus services linking Long Marston with both terminals, call Harrogate 01532 566061. For details of National Express coach links to York, call 01532 460011.

# 12
# RAF MARSTON MOOR
## 1941–5

## *Introduction*

Britain's unpreparedness for war in 1939 has constituted a much-laboured point – to an extent which has resulted in an overstatement of the case. For example, during the inter-war years the number of military airfields in the British Isles doubled – to a total of 116. The initial problem, as far as all branches of the armed forces were concerned, lay in trying to convince the politicians successfully that a second world war would not be fought on the same terms as the First World War. Thus, the RAF was compelled to operate from grass airfields. When it became clear that in wet weather heavy bombers would sink in the mud, work started on the provision of hard runways, which consisted of often poor foundations topped with a thin layer of tarmac. It was not until late in the day that concrete was recognized as providing the most suitable runway surface. Also underestimated at the beginning was the length of runway a heavy bomber would need. At first, a main runway length of 1,000 yards was considered sufficient – a figure which would require drastic revision.

Before anything could be done, it was essential to locate an adequate site. The south of England had been home to most airfields during the First World War when the theatre of operations was limited to France. But in the 1930s, and with foresight, it was recognized that in the event of another war, it would be possible to despatch bombers into the heart of Germany with more ease if airfields were constructed in the north of England. This strategy was coupled with a complete overhaul of the old system of area commands. The Air Defence of Great Britain now became no less than four separate bodies – Fighter Command, Bomber Command, Coastal Command and Training Command – all of which competed for resources and glory, though not necessarily in that order.

For consideration as a potential military airfield, a site had to be flat, occupying land not more than 650 ft above sea-level, and planners had to ensure that stations were placed not less than 3 miles apart. Each site required a minimum of 700 acres. For every proposed site that was approved, there would be up to a dozen rejected.

Second World War military airfields in Yorkshire – the country which was to become home to Bomber Command's No. 4 Group and the Royal Canadian Air Force's No. 6 Group – were located largely on the Plain of Holderness to the north and west of Hull, and throughout the length and breadth of the Vale of York. As these were areas of significant food production, agricultural interests had to be considered. For example, a proposal for an airfield at Appleton Wiske near Northallerton in the North Riding of Yorkshire was rejected on the grounds that construction would seriously disrupt agricultural production in the area. Proposals for a Bomber Command airfield at Strensall, to the north-east of York, failed for similar reasons.

As a location for military airfields, Yorkshire had a fair pedigree. Even before 1914, much pioneering aviation work had taken place in the county and, despite the early proliferation of airfields in the south, the Royal Flying Corps had operated from several Yorkshire bases such as Beverley and Driffield in the First World War.

And when, on the brink of another war, surveying teams were searching for likely future sites in Yorkshire, they identified as quite promising the area to the immediate west of York. Between York and the village of Long Marston, the landscape was undulating but, beyond Long Marston, in the locality of the village of Tockwith, it levelled out to a degree which convinced the surveyors that here was a site with scope for development.

# The Road to RAF Marston Moor

Eventually RAF Marston Moor would have three concrete runways. The main runway was 6,000 ft in length, with two subsidiaries of 4,200 ft each. The main aerodrome site fitted snugly into a triangle formed by the north-western portion of the airfield perimeter road, the Rudgate Roman road and the Long Marston–Cowthorpe road. There were six hangars in this area, all of the T2 type. These were mass-produced structures, 240 ft long and 115 ft wide, giving a total of thirty-two aircraft bays. Bordering the perimeter road, between the hangars and the main runway, was the watch tower. As with aircraft sheds, there were several types. Marston Moor's watch tower was type 518/40, a popular design which one readily associates with Second World War airfields – a two-storey structure with an interior stairway to the rear.

WAAF Officers' Mess, RAF Marston Moor. There is much work to be done in ensuring the preservation of such valuable examples of wartime airfield architecture.

In the south-west corner of the main airfield site, suitably isolated, were the bomb stores. In addition to being set apart from the aerodrome buildings and the domestic sites, the stores were dispersed within the storage area – heavy and light bombs, smoke bombs, incendiary bombs and so on, all connected by an intricate network of roads. To the east of the bomb stores was situated a single B1 hangar, a steel-framed corrugated iron structure with a pent roof. Moving anti-clockwise up towards Tockwith, and bordering the village itself, were the Aircraft Armament Stores.

When operating at capacity it was expected that RAF Marston Moor would be relatively densely populated, with 206 Officers, 744 Senior Non-Commissioned Officers and 1,164 Ordinary Ratings. In addition, there would be 12 WAAF Officers, 20 SNCO WAAFs and 326 OR WAAFs, making a grand total of 2,472 military personnel – easily dwarfing the combined population of all the surrounding villages. At airfields developed during the 1930s living accommodation had been well designed and sturdily built, but the necessity for rapid wartime expansion coupled with a shortage of materials led to a lowering of standards and to reliance upon the infamous Nissen Hut, a prefabricated cylindrical-shaped building of corrugated steel, named after its designer, Lieutenant-Colonel Peter Nissen.

At Marston Moor, two main WAAF sites were constructed along a farm track to the north of Tockwith Lane and the aerodrome site. In 1942 it became the norm on newly constructed airfields for dining halls and officers' and sergeants' messes to be shared between RAF and WAAF personnel. At Marston Moor, however, the WAAFs had their own messes, dining-hall and NAAFI facilities.

A little further to the west, towards the Rudgate crossroads, were additional RAF personnel communal sites comprising living-quarters and such mundane yet essential items as ablution and latrine facilities. The Sick Quarters site, with facilities for only twenty-five patients, was positioned at the crossroads itself and included an ambulance garage and mortuary.

To the south of the Tockwith road, domestic sites Nos 1, 2, 3 and 4 had the advantage of being rather less exposed, with woodland being used as camouflage. The dispersed sites extended almost to Cowthorpe, the western perimeter being marked by the Wireless-Telegraph site – a distance of 1½ miles from the aerodrome. Nearest to the aerodrome, off a track running parallel with Rudgate was Communal Site No. 1. In addition to the usual buildings, this site included a squash court and gymnasium, a grocery store, and barbers', shoemakers' and tailors' shops. Every site had its own air-raid shelter.

In such a way – and at a cost of around £500,000 – was the rural landscape in the vicinity of the sleepy village of Tockwith transformed during the early months of 1941.

# RAF Marston Moor (1941–5)

RAF Marston Moor began life on 20 November 1941 as part of Bomber Command's Yorkshire No. 4 Group as a conversion training station. At the outbreak of war, the RAF had a relatively poor selection of bombers. For example, there was the Wellington with a maximum speed of around 250 mph and a maximum bomb load of 4,500 lb, with a range of 1,200 miles, and the Blenheim, a light bomber, with a top speed of around 260 mph, carrying fuel for 1,460 miles with a bomb load of 1,000 lb. Both were lightly armed. The better armed Hampden, with a top speed of 243 mph and a range of 1,200 miles, could carry a bomb load of 4,000 lb. However, Wellington, Blenheim and Hampden were all twin-engined aircraft. (There was even accelerated production of a single-engined bomber, the Battle, generally regarded as obsolete as early as 1933.) Designs for four-engined heavy bombers had been in the pipeline for several years, but it was not at first considered prudent to disrupt existing production schedules. In the

Handley Page Halifax II (W7676 TL–P) of No. 35 Squadron, based at RAF Marston Moor. Although a vast improvement on the cumbersome four-engined Stirling, the Halifax suffered heavy losses and was, in turn, superseded by the incomparable Lancaster. (RAF Museum, Hendon)

first year of war, almost 500 bombers were lost, and quantity rather than quality was the byword.

However, by the middle of 1941 the new Halifax bomber was rolling off the production line. It took far longer to build a Halifax than it did to build any of its twin-engined predecessors, but the finished product was far superior to anything that Bomber Command had at its disposal. In its final version, the four-engined Halifax was capable of carrying a bomb load of 13,000 lb, with sufficient fuel to give it a range of 1,000 miles. It was also heavily armed, with .303 machine-guns operating from a mid-upper turret as well as front and rear turrets. In time, the Halifax itself would be superseded by the Lancaster but, in 1941, it was received gratefully by the No. 4 Group as the state of the art.

Retraining presented a whole new range of problems, for experienced pilots had to be taken out of the line at a time of mounting losses. What was sometimes literally a three-week 'crash course' was undertaken by pilots who could lose their lives in struggling to become proficient in handling an aircraft which had a wingspan of 104 ft as against the 56 ft of a Blenheim.

By 1943 the Halifax was well established and the training function of

Marston Moor was benefiting from the experience of its station commander, Group Captain Leonard Cheshire. Although Cheshire remained at Marston Moor for a few months only – later going on to head the 617 'Dambusters' Squadron – his term of office was a productive one. With its heavy bomb loads, a Halifax flying into the heart of Germany would have very little fuel to spare on the return journey, and Cheshire was able to provide invaluable advice on the subject of economical cruising heights. He also noticed that the loss of one of its four engines could cause the Halifax to spin out of control. He attributed the phenomenon to a problem with the rudder design – a claim which, although it proved correct, infuriated the manufacturers.

In addition to heavy bombers, fighter aircraft – Spitfires and Hurricanes – were also housed at Marston Moor from time to time. Before the war, the concept of fighter escorts for bombers had been disregarded. Indeed, bitter rivalry between Fighter and Bomber Commands precluded much in the way of cooperation, and it took repeated heavy losses for Bomber Command to admit that some measure of protection was needed against the deadly German Me 109s. Subsequent events were to demonstrate the importance of fighter-escorted sorties, for although casualties among both bombers and fighters remained high, the life blood was being drained from the Luftwaffe, which suffered staggering losses during the final months of the war.

# The Aftermath

The war in Europe drew to a close on 7 May 1945, Hitler having committed suicide a week before, on 30 April. Although Britain celebrated VE-Day (Victory in Europe) on 8 May, the war in the Far East dragged on. Even after the atomic bombing of Hiroshima and Nagasaki, the Japanese refused to capitulate. Finally, on 2 September, representatives of the Japanese government assembled on the USS *Missouri* to sign the instrument of surrender – and 2 September became VJ-Day (Victory over Japan).

In fact, for practical purposes, the war in the air had been over for some time. From the autumn of 1944 RAF Bomber Command was spoiled for choice of targets. One school of thought advocated a concentration of bombing raids on Germany's oil fields while another, led by Arthur Harris, felt that Germany could be brought to its knees by a blitz on the major cities. In fact, neither strategy was likely to win the war. Legendary German efficiency resulted in minimal disruption of production where industrial targets were concerned, while, as in the London blitz of 1940–1, the bombing of civilian targets seemed to have the effect of strengthening morale. (After the war, Albert Speer, German Minister of Armaments, was encouraged to support Harris's viewpoint.)

Throughout the final months of the war, Bomber Command's losses remained heavy. In 1945 over 600 aircraft were lost – almost as many as in the darkest year of 1940. Of course, production had increased and the American 8th Air Force was now taking a lot of the strain. Thus, Halifax Mk IIIs and Hurricane Mk IVs were beginning to filter through to airfields such as Marston Moor.

During the immediate post-war months most United Kingdom airfields remained operational. There was no immediate shut-down at Marston Moor and aircraft continued to arrive. Although losses through enemy action had ceased, there were still many accidental deaths. Not until November 1945 did Marston Moor close. For many hundreds of bases like Marston Moor, the future was uncertain. The station's ex-commander, Leonard Cheshire, had plans to develop the facilities along the lines of 'model' villages, providing homes and work for ex-servicemen, a worthy scheme which never materialized. Some buildings, including watch towers, were converted into accommodation by individuals in need of housing. Gypsies still congregate on sites around the country.

Owners of properties in the vicinity of airfields – some in the middle of sites, as at Marston Moor – were able to return to peace-time activities. Until 1988, the Home Office used the Marston Moor hangars for storage. At the time of writing (1994), some of the land has been returned to agricultural use, while the hangars are still used for storage by businesses. Also, part of the runway system has been utilized for specialized driver training – an activity located on many airfields during the 1950s.

In his definitive book *Britain's Military Airfields 1939–45*, David J. Smith concludes that wartime airfield development 'has left an imprint on the landscape which will be discernible for centuries'. It is feared, however, that this is a somewhat optimistic appraisal of the situation. Gradually, the remains of many airfields are disappearing under such projects as housing developments and road improvement schemes. Within the foreseeable future, the remnants of RAF Marston Moor's domestic sites may disappear. The hangars may remain by virtue of their value as warehousing, and the industrial estate development on the western edge of the main aerodrome site has set an example for others to follow. Unfortunately, a sadly lacking standardized measure of protection is needed. In this connection, it is worthy of note that English Heritage's proposed register of historic battlefields makes no mention of significant military airfields, an omission which renders the prospects for their survival beyond the turn of the century undeniably bleak.

# *The Walk*

**Distance:** 5 miles (8.05 km)

Begin in Tockwith at the Church of the Epiphany (point A; Pathfinder 664 466524). There is ample parking along the main street. Walk out of Tockwith on the Cowthorpe road. The main aerodrome site soon looms up on the left. Continue walking to Blind Lane (point B). Turn right into Blind Lane. A little way up on the left-hand side – and now converted to light industrial use – are the remains of WAAF Site No. 2 (Pathfinder 664 456533).

Of greater interest, because it is rather more intact, is WAAF Site No. 1, further along on the opposite side of the lane (Pathfinder 664 458534). A good overall view of the site can be obtained by looking over the fields from the lane as one approaches. The most prominent feature of the scene today is a modern dwelling – an incongruous addition to the scene. The first hut one sees, bordering the road, is the picket post and detention room. At the other side of the entrance is the well-preserved WAAF Officers' Mess. Both buildings are of the Type B variety – timber-framed with a projected life span of only a few years, yet despite over half a century of neglect, many such temporary huts remain.

Return to the main road and turn to the right. Immediately opposite are two fine T2 hangars, dominating the landscape. The grass verge nearest the hangars provides good walking. A footpath is available for a portion of the route along the road. Footpaths often border airfields and constitute a valuable surviving wartime addition to the landscape. Beyond the crossroads, turn left into Moorside (point C).

On the left are the remains of Communal Site No. 1 (Pathfinder 664 447526). Within recent years, much damage has been wrought by the adaptation of the site to a warehousing function although further along, towards the farm, the complex has been less disturbed.

Just past Moor Side Farm, the track veers off to the left, over Ainstey Beck. A straight walk ends at the Rudgate Roman road. Turn left and walk up to the main airfield entrance (point D), clearly indicated by the surviving water tower. In company with many main airfield sites, this area has been converted to industrial estate usage. It is not often, however, that one meets with a site where efforts have been made to retain the character of the original. RAF Marston Moor had a most attractive entrance – and it remains so, with a tree-lined curving road leading into the camp. The well preserved guard house to the left of the entrance is now the estate office, where one should call if one wishes to wander inside.

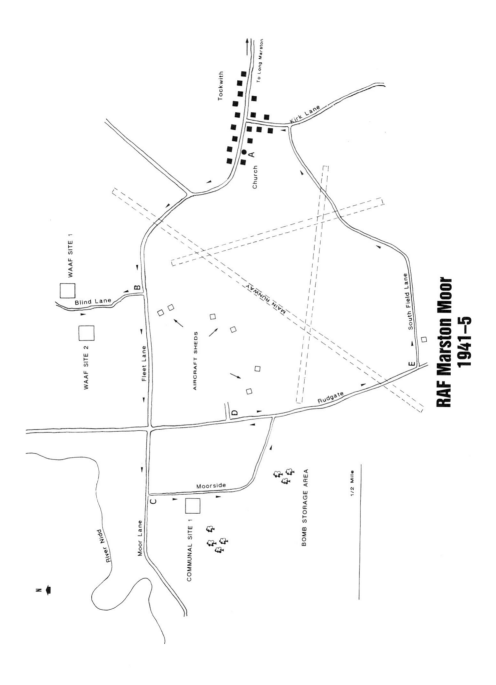

# RAF Marston Moor
# 1941–5

To Long Marston

Tockwith

Church

A

Kirk Lane

WAAF SITE 1

Blind Lane

B

WAAF SITE 2

Fleet Lane

AIRCRAFT SHEDS

MAIN RUNWAY

D

Rudgate

E

South Field Lane

Moorside

C

COMMUNAL SITE 1

Moor Lane

River Nidd

BOMB STORAGE AREA

1/2 Mile

N

Aircraft sheds, RAF Marston Moor. Bordering Fleet Lane to the west of Tockwith, these two T2 type hangars, once capable of housing twenty-three aircraft, still perform a storage function, albeit one more in keeping with peace-time activities, over half a century after their construction.

It is now necessary to retrace one's steps down Rudgate. Although quite straight, as one would imagine because of its Roman origins, a little care has to be exercised when walking along it as it lacks an adequate grass verge. As one leaves the main airfield site behind, a glance over to the left gives a good middle-distance view of the watch tower.

On the right, the area occupied by the bomb stores comes into view. As might be expected, the concrete bunker-like structures survive. Further along Rudgate, a glance to the right and left reveals the remains of the main runway. Often, the construction of an airfield would lead to the removal of roads in a particular locality. At this point, Rudgate was obliterated, the land it occupied being requisitioned for runway construction purposes.

Rudgate takes up its course once more at the junction with South Field Lane (point E). Turn into South Field Lane, to walk past another hangar – this time, a B1. The walk up South Field Lane is an uneventful one, punctuated only by the occasional sad pile of rubble.

At the top of South Field Lane, turn left into Kirk Lane and back into Tockwith, where refreshment at the Boot and Shoe will be in order before returning to the starting-point.

# Further Explorations

It is not unusual to find military airfields adjacent to historic battlefield sites. Marston Moor abuts on a Civil War site, as do the airfields at Chalgrove and Edgehill. (Similarly, Full Sutton is adjacent to the battlefield of Stamford Bridge – and so on.) Thus, it is often possible to explore two battlefields simultaneously. Alternatively, one may prefer to compare and contrast two or more military airfields, a task which may be undertaken by an exploration of an airfield and its affiliated stations.

One airfield which was to become a sub-station of RAF Marston Moor was situated at Acaster Malbis (Landranger 105 5742). Four miles to the south of York and 10 miles away from Tockwith, Acaster Malbis is easily accessible via the A63 – the airfield being positioned to the south of the village. (It was at Acaster Malbis, it may be remembered, that the Parliamentarian forces about to lay siege to York constructed their bridge of boats to take them across the Ouse.)

In the early part of 1942 RAF Acaster Malbis opened for business as home to a fighter squadron. Later in the year, it was turned over to Flying Training Command which, in turn, pulled out in January 1943. Although splendidly level, on the flood-plain of the Ouse, the site was often engulfed in heavy winter mists – a hazard common to areas bordering upon Yorkshire rivers – and, following several accidents, both Fighter Command and Flying Training Command considered it unsafe to continue using the facility. Despite these decisions, Bomber Command decided to move in, and three concrete runways were constructed on what had hitherto functioned as a grass airfield.

Despite the valuable wartime resources invested in the creation of a bomber station, no bombers ever flew from Acaster Malbis. Doubtless, the planners realized the errors of their ways, albeit at a late stage in the proceedings and from late 1943 until its closure in 1946, it was used for storage, maintenance and non-flying training.

Acaster Malbis is of interest today (1994) because it is possible to walk around the perimeter, which is now a public footpath, in addition to walking across the centre via the minor road, closed when the airfield was under construction, and since reopened. The watch tower, backed by one of the aircraft sheds – a T2 hangar – has survived (Pathfinder 673 575432), as has a portion of Communal Site No. 4, including the officers' mess (Pathfinder 673 571438) and sergeants' mess (Pathfinder 673 569437).

During its early days several flying accidents occurred, which may explain why the airfield has a reputation for being haunted, with reported sightings of ghostly figures in flying gear appearing out of the mist.

Another sub-station of RAF Marston Moor was Riccall (Landranger 105 6137) Again, uncannily, the area has a connection with an historical battlefield, for it was at Riccall that the Norwegians moored their fleet prior to the battles of Fulford and Stamford Bridge.

Riccall opened as a Bomber Command station during the latter half of 1942 as a training ground for air-crews transferring from the twin-engined Wellingtons to the four-engined Halifax bombers. There were many accidents but, strangely enough, few seem to have been attributed to mist. Many airfields were situated on the flood-plains of Yorkshire rivers, but only Acaster Malbis appears to have been criticized for the choice of site.

At the end of the war, along with many other airfields, Riccall was not immediately abandoned by the RAF, being used for storage until its return of the land to its pre-war agricultural function in 1946. There is little left to see, although Communal Site No. 1 (Pathfinder 685 648357) including the gymnasium and airmen's dining-room, has survived.

# Further Information

A useful resume of wartime activity at RAF Marston Moor is to be found in Bruce Barrymore Halpenny's *Action Stations: Military Airfields of Yorkshire*. Detailed plans of the airfield – an invaluable aid to further exploration – may be obtained from the Royal Air Force Museum at Hendon (tel: 0181 205 2266).

Ordnance Survey maps for the area are Landranger 105 and Pathfinder 664.

The village of Tockwith features in the suggested walk relating to the Battle of Marston Moor (1644), and arrangements for reaching both sites are similar. Motorists should approach Tockwith from York via the B1224 or from the A1, either by taking the B1224 or via a minor road leading directly to Tockwith which joins the A1 2 miles further north. Mainline Rail terminals are at Harrogate (tel: 01532 448133) and York (tel: 01904 642155). For details of bus services linking Tockwith with both terminals, call Harrogate, 01532 566061. For details of National Express coach links to York, call 01532 460011.

# FURTHER READING

Place of publication given only if outside London.

General background reading:

Churchill, Winston S. *A History of the English-Speaking Peoples: The Birth of Britain*, Cassell & Co. Ltd, 1956.
——. *A History of the English-Speaking Peoples: The New World*, Cassell & Co. Ltd, 1956.

For more detailed background reading, see:

Adam, R.J. *A Conquest of England: The Coming of the Normans*, Hodder & Stoughton, 1965.
Bryant, Arthur. *The Age of Chivalry*, Collins, 1963.
Clarendon, Earl of. *The History of the Great Rebellion*, Oxford University Press, Oxford, 1967.
Compton, Piers. *Harold the King*, Robert Hale, 1951.
Davis, H.C.W. *England Under the Normans and the Angevins*, Methuen, 1961.
Froissart, Jean. *Chronicles*, Dent, 1906.
Fryde, Natalie. *The Tyranny and Fall of Edward II 1321–1326*, Cambridge University Press, Cambridge, 1979.
Jacob, E.F. *Oxford History of England: The Fifteenth Century 1399–1485*, Oxford University Press, Oxford, 1961.
Magnusson, Magnus and Palsson, Herman (trans.). *King Harald's Saga*, Penguin, 1966.
McKisack, May. *Oxford History of England: The Fourteenth Century 1307–1399*, Oxford University Press, Oxford, 1959.
Prestwich, Michael. *War and State in England 1272–1377*, Weidenfeld & Nicolson, 1980.
Wedgewood, C.V. *The King's Peace 1637–1641*, Collins, 1955.

For reading relating to Scotland and border warfare, see:

Mackie, J.D. *A History of Scotland*, Penguin, 1964.
Prebble, John. *The Lion in the North*, Secker and Warburg, 1971.

For reading relating to the Wars of the Roses, the following are recommended:

Chrimes, S.B. *Lancastrians, Yorkists and Henry VII*, Macmillan & Co. Ltd, 1964.

Lander, J.R. *The Wars of the Roses*, Alan Sutton Publishing Limited, Stroud, 1990.

Ross, Charles. *The Wars of the Roses: A Concise History*, Thames & Hudson, 1976.

For reading relating to the English Civil War, the following are recommended:

Ashley, M. *The English Civil War*, Alan Sutton Publishing Limited, Stroud, 1990.

Downing, T. and Millman, M. *Civil War*, Collins & Brown Ltd, 1991.

Kenyon, John. *The Civil Wars of England*, Weidenfeld & Nicolson, 1988.

For accounts of specific battles discussed in the text, see:

Knightly, Charles. *Flodden: The Anglo-Scottish War of 1513*, Almark Publishing, 1975.

Newman, Peter. *The Battle of Marston Moor*, Antony Bird, Chichester, 1981.

Wenham, Peter. *The Great and Close Siege of York 1644*, Roundwood Press, Kineton, 1970.

Young, Peter. *Marston Moor 1644: The Campaign and the Battle*, Roundwood Press, Kineton, 1970.

For general accounts of British battles, see:

Baker, Antony. *A Battlefield Atlas of the English Civil War*, Ian Allan Ltd, 1986.

Barrett, C.R.B. *Battles and Battlefields in England*, A.D. Innes & Co., 1896.

Bennett, Martyn. *Traveller's Guide to the Battlefields of the English Civil War*, Webb & Bower, 1990.

Brooke, Richard. *Visits to Fields of Battle in England in the Fifteenth Century*, A.J. Sutton, Dursley, 1975.

Burne, Alfred H. *The Battlefields of England*, Methuen & Co. Ltd, 1950.

——. *More Battlefields of England*, Methuen & Co. Ltd, 1952.

Fairbairn, Neil. *A Traveller's Guide to the Battlefields of Britain*, Evans Brothers, 1983.

Graham, Frank. *Famous Northern Battles*, Butler Publishing, Northumberland, 1988.

Green, Howard. *Guide to the Battlefields of Britain and Ireland*, Constable & Co. Ltd, 1973.

Halpenny, Bruce Barrymore. *Action Stations: Military Airfields of Yorkshire*, Patrick Stephens, Wellingborough, 1982.

Kinross, John, *The Battlefields of Britain*, David & Charles, Newton Abbot, 1979.

Leadman, Alex D.H. *Battles Fought in Yorkshire*, 1891.

Newman, P.R. *Atlas of the English Civil War*, Croom Helm, 1985.

Rogers, Colonel H.C.B. *Battles & Generals of the Civil Wars 1642–1651*, Seeley Service & Co. Ltd, 1968.

Seymour, William. *Battles in Britain 1066–1547*, Sidgwick & Jackson, 1975.

——. *Battles in Britain 1642–1746*, Sidgwick & Jackson, 1975.

Smith, David J. *Britain's Military Airfields 1939–45*, Patrick Stephens, Wellingborough, 1989.

Smurthwaite, David. *The Complete Guide to the Battlefields of Britain*, Michael Joseph Ltd, 1993.

Warner, David. *British Battlefields: The North*, Osprey Publishing Ltd, 1972.

——. *British Battlefields: Scotland and the Borders*, Osprey Publishing Ltd, 1975.

Wedgewood, C.V. *Civil War Battlefields*, BBC, date not known.

Wetherell, J.E. *Fields of Fame in England and Scotland*, Macmillan, Toronto, 1923.

Woolrych, Austin. *Battles of the English Civil War*, Batsford, 1961.

Young, Peter and Adair, John. *From Hastings to Culloden*, Roundwood Press, Kineton, 1979.

Young, Peter and Emberton, Wilfrid. *Sieges of the Great Civil War*, Bell & Hyman, 1978.

For general guides to the counties covered by this volume, see:

Gaunt, Peter. *The Cromwellian Gazeteer*, Alan Sutton Publishing Limited, Stroud, 1992.

Mee, Arthur. *The King's England: Northumberland*, Hodder & Stoughton, 1964 ed.

——. *The King's England: Durham*, Hodder & Stoughton, 1969 ed.

——. *The King's England: Yorkshire – North Riding*, Hodder & Stoughton, 1969 ed.

——. *The King's England: Yorkshire – East Riding with York*, Hodder & Stoughton, 1964 ed.

——. *The King's England: Yorkshire – West Riding*, Hodder & Stoughton, 1969 ed.

For an excellent all-round introduction to walking and rambling, see:

Westacott, H.D. *The Walker's Handbook*, Oxford Illustrated Press, Yeovil, 1980.

# INDEX OF PLACES

Aberdeen, 103
Acaster Malbis, 148
Aldborough, 33, 34, 36
Alnwick, 50, 77, 79, 81, 91
Ancrum Moor, 94
Appleton Wiske, 139
Arundel, 18
Aydon Castle, 87

Bamburgh, 77, 82
Bannockburn, 26
Bearpark, 41
Berkeley Castle, 27, 31
Berwick-upon-Tweed, 35, 64, 98, 99, 103, 104
Beverley, 10, 139
Bilborough, 74
Bishop Auckland, 40
Bishopthorpe, 34
Blakehope, 60
Blanchland, 84
Bolton, 127
Bolton Percy, 74
Boroughbridge, 25–36 *passim*, 128
Bradford, 125
Braham Moor, 136, 137
Brancepeth, 48, 52
Branxton, 92, 97
Brest, 90
Bridlington, 114, 115
Bristol, 16, 18, 19
Brough, 112
Burford, 64
Byland Abbey, 31
Bywell Castle, 83

Caen, 38
Calais, 38, 43, 90
Carlaverlock Castle, 107

Carlisle, 16, 38, 52
Castleford, 64
Catterick, 22, 112, 124
Cawood, 73, 74, 129, 130
Chalgrove, 131, 148
Chatillon, 37
Cheriton, 127
Chester, ix
Chesters Fort, 86
Cirencester, 27
Clitheroe, 83
Coldstream, 91, 104
Cologne, 31
Corbridge, 40, 84, 86
Corfe Castle, 18
Coventry, 27
Cowthorpe, 139
Crookham, 98
Cropredy Bridge, 127

Dalkeith, 103
Darlington, 17, 19
Dawston in Liddesdale, ix
Derby, 27
Dilston Castle, 87
Doncaster, 27, 112
Driffield, 9, 115, 139
Dumbarton, 103, 104
Dunbar, 103
Dunstanburgh, 28, 77, 81
Durham, 40, 42, 45, 47, 48, 49, 52, 91

Edgehill, 34, 125, 148
Edinburgh, 103, 107
Elsdon, 60, 61
Etal, 91, 98, 99
Evesham, 131
Exeter, 15

Ferry Hill, 40
Ferrybridge, 64, 66, 71
Finchale Priory, 48
Flodden, ix, 89–100 *passim*
Ford, 91, 98, 100
Fountains Abbey, 21
Fulford, 4, 9, 11, 115
Full Sutton, 11, 148

Gloucester, 63

Halton, 87
Harlech, 62
Harrogate, 136
Healaugh, 136
Heddon-on-the-Wall, 110
Hegeley Moor, 79, 80, 81
Hereford, 31, 63
Hexham, ix, 40, 76–88 *passim*
Holyrood, 101
Homildon Hill, 57
Hull, 62, 74, 115, 139

Jedburgh, 52

Kelso, 103
Kenilworth, 27, 31
Kilham, 115
Kirk Merrington, 40
Knaresborough, 33, 35, 127, 128, 136

Lanercost Priory, 40
Leeds, 130
Leeds Castle (Kent), 26, 27
Leeming, 23
Lichfield, 27
Lincoln, 19, 112
Liverpool, 127
London, 4, 27, 44, 64, 83, 98, 114, 127, 143
Long Marston, 133, 125–37 *passim*
Ludworth, 49
Lumley Castle, 48

Marston Moor, ix, x, 35, 103, 117, 118, 121, 125, 125–37 *passim*

Middlethorpe, 115
Milford, 92
Minskip, 36
Mortimer's Cross, 63, 64, 76
Mount Grace Priory, 22
Myton-on-Swale, 34

Nantwich, 127
Naseby, 35, 131
Newark, 115, 116, 127
Newburn, ix, 101–11 *passim*, 126
Newcastle, 52, 56, 79, 80, 81, 91, 104, 105, 106, 110
Newstead, 60
Newton Kyme, 74
Norham Castle, 77, 79, 91, 98, 99
Northallerton, 13–24 *passim*, 35, 139
Northampton, 62
Nun Appleton, 74
Nun Monkton, 137

Otterburn, 40, 50–61 *passim*
Oxford, 26, 114

Pevensey, 7
Pinkie Cleugh, 94
Pittington, 49
Poitiers, 37, 44
Pontefract, 11, 28, 30, 34, 35, 64, 91
Poppleton, 115, 128
Portsmouth, 15
Preston, ix
Prudhoe, 110

Riccall, 4, 6, 10, 11, 149
Rievaulx Abbey, 21
Ripley Castle, 136
Ripon, 107, 136
Rochester, 60
Roxburgh, 41
Ryton, 105, 109

St Albans, 64, 76
St Andrews, 101
Sandwich, 3, 4
Saxton, 66, 67, 71

Scarborough, 16, 26, 117
Scrivelsby, 99
Selby, 115
Sheen, 95
Sheriff Hutton, 10, 11, 48
Shrewsbury, 27, 54, 57, 127
Solway Moss, 94
South Cave, 118
Southampton, 15
Stamford Bridge, ix, x, 1–12 *passim*, 29, 148
Stockport, 127
Strensall, 24, 139
Sunderland Bridge, 40

Tadcaster, 5, 68, 71, 74, 112, 129
Thirsk, 15
Thornton Bridge, 128

Tockwith, 129, 139–49 *passim*
Towton, 62–75 *passim*, 76, 82
Tutbury, 27

Wakefield, ix, 63, 64, 69, 72
Wallingford, 27
Wark, 91, 98, 99
Weymouth, 43
Whitby, 50, 115
Whitley Chapel, 84, 86
Wooler, 91
Worcester, 118
Worksop, 63

York, x, 4, 5, 7, 10, 11, 12, 16, 22, 60, 64, 69, 79, 80, 91, 103, 106, 107, 108, 112–24 *passim*, 127, 128, 130, 148

# INDEX OF PERSONS

Abergavenny, Lord (John Hastings), 27
Albermarle, Earl of (William le Gros), 16
Alfred the Great (King of the English), 1
Argyll, 2nd Earl of (Archibald Campbell), 92, 93
Argyll, 8th Earl of (Archibald Campbell), 125
Astley, Sir Jacob, 95
Audley, Hugh (the elder), 27
Audley, Hugh (the younger), 27

Badlesmere, Bartholomew, 26, 27
Baillie, Lieutenant-General William, 130
Balliol, Bernard de, 16
Balliol, Edward, 38, 41
Balliol, John (King of Scotland), 110
Becket, Thomas, 35
Bellasyse, Lord John, 115
Berkeley, Maurice, 27
Bothwell, 2nd Earl of (Adam Hepburn), 92, 93
Bowles, Edward, 118
Breze, Pierre de, 77, 83
Bulmer, Bertram de, 10
Byron, 1st Lord (John), 129

Charles I (King of England), 101, 102, 103, 104, 106, 107, 110, 111, 114, 118, 125, 126, 127, 131, 133
Charles IV (King of France), 31, 37
Charles VIII (King of France), 90
Cheshire, Group Captain Leonard, 143
Chester, 2nd Earl of (Ranulf), 19
Clifford, 9th Baron, 62, 64, 66, 71
Clifford, Sir Roger, 28, 29
Constable, Sir William, 115
Crawford, Colonel, 116
Crawford, 6th Earl of (John Lindsay), 92

Conway, Lord, 105, 106
Copeland, John, 39, 41, 43, 44
Cromwell, Oliver, 74, 99, 110, 130, 131, 133, 134, 136
Culpeper, Thomas, 73
Curtois, Robert, 110

Dacre, 1st Baron (Ralph), 66, 67, 71, 72, 73
Dacre, 3rd Baron (Thomas), 92, 93, 94
Dalzell, Sir William, 52
D'Amory, Sir Roger, 27
Danby, Francis, 118
David I (King of Scotland), 15, 16, 17, 18
David II (King of Scotland), 38, 39, 40, 41, 43, 48, 51
Derwentwater, 3rd Earl of, 87
Derwentwater, Lady, 87
Despenser, Hugh, 26, 27, 30
Dorset, 2nd Marquis of (Thomas Grey), 90
Douglas, Archibald, 57
Douglas, 2nd Earl of (James), 51, 52, 53, 54, 55, 56
Douglas, Sir William, 40, 41, 52

Edward I (King of England), 1, 2, 25, 50, 110, 111
Edward II (King of England), 25, 27, 30, 31, 34, 43, 44, 73, 99, 111
Edward III (King of England), 37, 38, 136
Edward, Earl of March (afterwards King Edward III of England), 11, 64, 65, 66, 76, 77, 79, 80, 81, 83
Edward, Prince of Wales (son of Henry VI), 62, 83
Edwin (King of Northumbria), 112

Elizabeth I (Queen of England), 73
Elizabeth Woodville (Queen of Edward IV), 11
Exeter, Duke of (Henry Holland), 69
Eythin, Lord (James King), 129

Fairfax, 2nd Baron (Ferdinando), 115, 129, 130
Fairfax, Margaret, 137
Fairfax, Sir Thomas, 35, 74, 115, 116, 117, 119, 127, 129, 130, 134
Fauconberg, Lord (William Neville), 64, 66
Ferdinand (King of Aragon), 90
Fitzwalter, Lord, 64, 66
Flambard, Bishop, 99
Fleetwood, Lieutenant-General Charles, 118
Ford, Ordinel de, 100

Gaveston, Piers, 25
Geoffrey of Anjou, 14, 15
Gloucester, Earl of (Gilbert de Clare), 25
Gloucester, Earl of (Robert), 15, 16, 18, 19
Godwin, Earl, 1
Goring, Lord George, 129, 130
Graham, William, 41
Gray, Sir Thomas, 53
Grey of Ruthen, Lord (Edmund), 62
Grey, Sir Ralph, 77, 83

Hamilton, James, 1st Duke of, 102, 103, 126
Harcla, Sir Andrew de, 28, 29, 30, 31
Hardrada, Harald (King of Norway), 3, 4, 5, 6, 7, 11
Harold II (King of the English), 1, 2, 3, 4, 5, 6, 7, 9, 74
Harris, Air Marshall Sir Arthur, 143, 144
Hastings, Lord (Randolph), 43
Hatfield, Thomas (Bishop of Durham), 40
Hawkesworth, Walter, 118

Henderson, Alexander, 101, 102
Henrietta Maria (Queen of Charles I), 114
Henry I (King of England), 13, 21
Henry IV (King of England), 10, 22, 57, 136
Henry V (King of England), 90
Henry VI (King of England), 62, 64, 69, 73, 77, 78, 79, 80, 81, 83
Henry VII (King of England), 11, 89
Henry VIII (King of England), 73, 89, 90, 91, 95, 97, 124
Henry, Prince (son of David I), 16, 17, 18
Henry of Blois (Bishop of Winchester), 13, 14
Hereford, Earl of, 27, 28, 29
Heron, Sir William, 100
Heron, Lady, 100
Hitler, Adolf, 143
Holland, Robert, 27
Holland, Thomas (Duke of Surrey), 22
Home, 3rd Baron (Alexander), 92, 93, 97
Hope, Sir Thomas, 125
Howard, Edmund, 92, 93, 97
Howard, Catherine (Queen of Henry VIII), 73
Howard, Thomas, 91, 92, 95
Hudson, George, 123
Hungerford, Lord, 79, 81
Huntley, 3rd Earl of (Alexander Gordon), 92, 93
Hussey, Sir Thomas, 81

Ingilby, Jane, 136
Ingilby, Sir Thomas, 136
Ingilby, Sir William, 136
Ingilby, Lady, 136
Isabella (Queen of Edward II), 31, 37

James I (King of England), 101, 114
James III (King of Scotland), 77
James IV (King of Scotland), 89, 91, 92, 95, 98, 99, 100
James V (King of Scotland), 95
Johnson, Archibald, 101, 102

Lambert, Major-General John, 115, 118
Lancaster, Earl of (Henry), 31
Lancaster, Earl of (Thomas), 25, 27, 28, 29, 30, 31, 33, 38
Lennox, Earl of (Matthew Stuart), 92, 93
Leslie, Alexander (afterwards Lord Leven), 23, 103, 104, 106, 109, 115, 118, 125, 126, 127, 129
Leslie, General Sir David, 129, 130, 133, 134
L'Espec, Walter, 16, 21
Louix XI (King of France), 76
Louis XII (King of France), 90
Ludwig IV (German Emperor), 37
Lumsden, Major-General Sir James, 130

Malcolm III (King of Scotland), 4
Manchester, 2nd Earl of (Edward Montague), 116, 128, 129, 130
Manners, Sir Robert de, 99
Margaret of Anjou (Queen of Henry VI), 62, 63, 64, 69, 76, 77, 78, 80, 83
Margaret Tudor (Queen of James IV of Scotland), 89
Marmion, Sir William, 99
Matilda (daughter of Henry I), 10, 13, 14, 15, 16, 18, 19
Melton, William (Archbishop of Canterbury), 34, 35
Monck, George (1st Duke of Albermarle), 74, 95, 118
Montagu, Lord (John Neville), 79, 80, 81, 83, 84
Montfort, Simon de, 30
Montgomery, Sir Hugh, 52, 55
Montgomery, Sir John, 52
Montrose, 5th Earl and 1st Marquis of (James Graham), 102, 104, 118, 126, 133
Montrose, 1st Earl of (William Graham), 92
Moray, Earl of (John Dunbar), 52
Morcar, Earl of Northumberland, 4
Mortimer, Roger, 31
'Mother Shipton', 136

Nevile, Francis, 118
Neville, George (Archbishop of York), 74
Neville, Ralph (4th Baron of Raby), 40, 41, 45
Newcastle, 1st Earl and 1st Marquis of (William Cavendish), 115, 116, 127, 128, 129, 130
Nissen, Lieutenant-Colonel Peter, 140
Norfolk, 1st Duke of (John Howard), 91
Norfolk, 3rd Duke of (John Mowbray), 66, 67, 71

Olaf (son of Harald Hardrada), 7
Oxford, 13th Earl of (John de Vere), 69

Paul, Earl of Orkney, 7
Pembroke, Earl of (William Herbert), 62, 63
Percy, Henry (1st Earl of Northumberland), 136
Percy, Henry (9th Baron and 2nd Lord of Alnwick), 40, 41
Percy, Henry (Hotspur), 52, 53, 54, 55, 56, 57
Percy, Sir Ralph (brother of Hotspur), 52, 53, 55
Percy, Sir Ralph (grandson of Hotspur), 77, 79, 80, 81
Philippa (Queen of Edward I), 43
Pym, John, 106, 126

Redvers, Baldwin de, 15, 18
Richard II (King of England), 10, 35, 51
Richard III (King of England), 11, 71, 72, 91, 124
Robert I, 'the Bruce' (King of Scotland), 38, 51
Robert, High Steward of Scotland (afterwards King Robert II of Scotland), 41, 44, 51
Rokeby, Sir Thomas, 41
Ros, Lord, 62, 79, 81
Roumane, William of, 19
Rupert, Prince, of the Rhine, 95, 116, 117, 127, 128, 129, 130, 131, 133, 134
Rutland, Earl of, 63

Saville, Sir William, 115
Simnel, Lambert, 89
Sinclair, Sir John, 55
Skippon, Major-General Philip, 95
Skirland, John, 94
Slingsby, Sir Henry, 35, 137
Somerset, 2nd Duke of (Edmund
    Beaufort), 62, 64, 66, 69, 76, 77, 79,
    80, 81, 82, 83
Speer, Albert, 144
Stanley, Sir Edward, 91, 93, 94, 95,
    98
Stephen (King of England), 10, 13, 14,
    15, 16, 18, 19, 21
Story, John, 118
Strafford, 1st Earl of (Thomas
    Wentworth), 104, 106, 116, 125
Surrey, Earl of (Thomas Howard), 90,
    91, 92, 93, 95, 98

Tailboys, Sir William, 81, 83
Talbot, Thomas, 83
Thurstan (Archbishop of York), 16, 21
Tostig (son of Earl Godwin), 1, 3, 4, 6,
    7
Trollope, Andrew, 64
Tudor, Owen, 63
Tyrell, Sir James, 89

Umfraville, Sir Robert de, 53, 54, 57
Umfraville, Sir Thomas de, 53, 54, 57

Vane, Sir Harry, 107

Waller, Sir William, 127
Walter, High Steward of Scotland, 51
Warbeck, Perkin, 89, 100
Ward, Sir Simon, 30
Warwick, 10th Earl of (Guy de
    Beauchamp), 26
Warwick, 14th Earl of (Richard Neville,
    'the Kingmaker'), 10, 64, 66, 69, 74,
    76, 81, 83, 89
Wentworth, Sir Thomas, 81
William I (King of England, 'the
    Conqueror'), 1, 3, 4, 7, 13, 14, 23, 50,
    110
William II (King of England), 13
Wilmot, Lieutenant-General Henry,
    106, 133
Wiltshire, Earl of, 63
Wolsey, Cardinal Thomas, 74

York, Duke of (Richard), 62, 63, 69

Zouche, William (Archbishop of York),
    40

Also available from Alan Sutton Publishing
by David Clark:

# Battlefield Walks
# The Midlands

*Battlefield Walks: The Midlands* provides a comprehensive collection of walks around the battlefield sites of middle England. Concentrating on the Wars of the Roses and the English Civil War, this illustrated volume describes in detail walks from just a few miles to over 10 miles in length.

The book takes the reader from Nottinghamshire to Northamptonshire, and from Warwickshire to Worcestershire, and from the hustle and bustle of Newark, to Bosworth Field, where Richard III lost his life and the Plantagenet line came to an end, and the tranquility of rural Naseby, where the conflicts of the English Civil War can be recalled. In all, sixteen walks are presented, each including helpful sketch maps, notes on transport connections, and suggestions for further explorations. Famous myths, mysteries and legends associated with the battles are recounted, and the text is illustrated with black and white photographs showing the places as they are today, as well as contemporary pictures of the historic events described.

An indispensible guide to the battlefields of the Midlands, this book will prove a stimulating and informative companion for the seasoned rambler, the military historian and for the family in search of an enjoyable day out in the English countryside.

0–7509–0258–2